The Transition Called Death

Cover art by *Jane A. Evans*

Illustrations by Terry Doerzaph

The Transition Called Death
A recurring experience

Charles Hampton

This publication made possible with
the assistance of the Kern Foundation
The Theosophical Publishing House
Wheaton, Ill. U.S.A.
Madras, India / London, England

Fifth printing. First Quest edition, 1979. Published by
the Theosophical Publishing House, a department of the
Theosophical Society in America.

Library of Congress Cataloging in Publication Data

Hampton, Charles, bp., 1886 -
  The transition called death, a recurring experience.

  First published in 1943 under title: Transition, a recurring experience.
  1. Death. 2. Theosophy. I. Title.
BP573.D4H3   1979   133.9'013   79-11056
ISBN 0-8356-0527-2

Printed in the United States of America

CONTENTS

There is no Death! What seems so is transition;
This life of mortal breath
Is but a suburb of the life elysian,
Whose portal we call Death.

Longfellow, *Resignation*—Stanza 5

FOREWORD

THE CONTEMPLATION OF DEATH

The mystery of death has always been one of the greatest challenges to the human mind. Perhaps many of us are in the position of the six-year-old who wrote in a letter to God, "What's it like to die? I just want to know. I don't want to do it." Yet, at the end, each one walks through the door of death alone, and the manner of his going is a uniquely private *mysterium.* Between dying and death— process and event—lies the journey of life, for the process begins with birth, while the event culminates each experience. It is only when we know we are dying that we begin contemplation of death.

Many religious traditions urge man to meditate upon death. Such contemplation is intended to serve as a reminder that man cannot, indeed must not, postpone decisions. Tibetan Buddhist texts, for example, suggest that in hesitating to decide on actions that will fulfill our humanity we risk the loss of our human status. Death, therefore, or the contemplation of death, does not point to the futility of life, but to its essential importance and value. An ancient work, *The Book of the Craft of Dying*, contains this admonition: "Against his will he dieth that hath not learned to die. Learn to die and thou shalt learn to live, for there shall none live that hath not learned to die." One of the oldest Chinese documents includes among the good fortunes promised to the man of virtue the finding of a death that will crown his life. That finding is dependent upon achieving skill in the process of dying. . . . Skill in the process of dying, however, lies for man in the achievement of a mind that is unafraid to contemplate death. Not long before the tragedy of his assassination, Dr. Martin Luther King, Jr. said, "A man is not really free until he has conquered the fear of death." And the Swiss psychologist, Dr. Carl Jung, once wrote: "Only he remains alive who is willing to die with life." What we need, surely, is a mind that can conquer death, not by abolishing the event (which would be analogous, as Alan Watts suggests, to effecting a cure for headache by chopping off one's head), but by facing the event without fear. The habitual readiness to meet without fear whatever occurs to us arises out of an attitude that accepts life as process, a process that includes both death and dying as natural, not outside the process of life but integral to it.

The problem of death is ultimately a problem of time, or rather of our consciousness of time. When life is accepted as process, we are not stuck in time, in the sense of *a* time, *this* time, today, tomorrow, or next year. How we experience death, as well as how we experience life, is determined by how we experience time. . . .

From time immemorial, the image of the hour-glass has served to symbolize the relation beween formalized time and death. This instrument, however, discloses the dialectic of the end, for it can be reversed, so that the sane begins to flow again toward a new beginning and another end. If this reversal is recognized, the image recalls the cosmic concept of time, whose fundamental form is the circle, symbol of recurrence, rebirth, and the process of life and death against the backdrop of eternity. So death becomes a birth, and birth a death; there occurs in consciousness a great revolution in which a spiritual recentering takes place. From that new center, the individual may say, as did the neophyte in the *Egyptian Book of the Dead:* "I am the Lord of the Stairs; I have made my nest on the borders of the sky." Or, as another ancient scripture puts it, "He who finds his way to the core of Self, whence rises all levels of the I, all spheres of the world, he who finds his way home to his first source . . . is born and reborn. Know that whoever is so born is the wisest of the wise; each moment of his life he is reborn anew."

. . . Kahlil Gibran may have said it best:

If you would indeed behold the spirit of death open your heart wide unto the body of life, For life and death are one, even as the river and the sea are one.

Joy Mills, *American Theosophist*,
Special Issue, Spring, 1973.

PREFACE

When anyone attempts to discuss the subject of life after death, it is quite reasonable to expect the question, "How do you know?"

The information given in this book is based on research covering no less than a quarter of a century. It is the result of first hand evidence from men and women who have actually passed through the experiences described and lived to give their testimony. Information known only to the departed has often been conveyed to the living by means of super-physical or extra-sensory perception.

Many people are now ready to agree with Schopenhauer who said: "The man who denies the fact of clairvoyance is not entitled to be called a sceptic, he is merely ignorant." Clairvoyance means "clear seeing" just as clairaudience means "clear hearing." The author himself has experienced this extra-sensory power and has known many others who have developed the necessary sensitivity which made it possible for them to investigate at first hand.

No one is asked to accept this evidence blindly.

It is a field which anyone may investigate for himself. Those who have first hand knowledge may be contradicted or ridiculed by others who are ignorant, but the Gnostic would not be disturbed by the Agnostic.

The early Church Fathers recognized that there was a science of unfolding faculties of the higher nature by means of self-discipline. By this technique spiritual truths are capable of reverification by each generation. Information obtained in this way is just as substantial as, let us say—astronomy. If a student is unwilling to study higher mathematics, gravitation, statics, magnetics and many other sub-divisions of astronomy, he might be willing to accept the word of experts in whom he has confidence, who have made such investigations.

Those for whom this book is intended and who are prepared for the reception of the truth it expresses will recognize and accept that truth.

CHARLES HAMPTON

ACKNOWLEDGMENT

Grateful acknowledgment is made to:
> The MacMillan Company,
> Methuen & Co., Ltd.,
> Harper & Brothers, Publishers,
> Dodd, Mead and Company and
> *The Atlantic Monthly*

for their gracious permission to quote briefly from the writings of J. W. Dunne, Gerald Heard, Maurice Maeterlinck, Hereward Carrington, and others.

Death is nothing to us, since when we are, death has not come, and when death has come, we are not.

Epicursus [341 — 270 B.C.], *Diogenes Laertius*, bx.Xm sec, 125.

1

EVIDENCE OF SURVIVAL

Our birth is but a sleep and a forgetting;
The Soul that rises with us, our life's Star,
Hath elsewhere had its setting,
And cometh from afar:
Not in entire forgetfulness,
And not in utter nakedness,
But trailing clouds of glory do we come
From God, who is our home.

William Wordsworth, *Intimations of Immortality*

Life in the physical world may be likened to an endless procession. Every minute of every day babies are being born, and every minute people die. This journey from birth to death has been going on for thousands, if not millions of years.

A person would have to be quite unintelligent if, at some period of his life, he did not wonder what happened after death and before birth. Where do all these dead people go? We see them no more—at least we do not see a physical form.

But there are many things we do not see, and many sounds we do not hear. We do not see nor hear the symphony travel from Philadelphia to Los Angeles, but that each separate note and melody is transmitted is a fact we cannot deny. We cannot

3

see, with ordinary physical sight, the etheric matter through which our radio programs travel, yet it is physical matter.

But some people can see etheric matter. Others can hear non-physical sounds and carry on conversations by means of telepathy with the miscalled "dead." We shall give examples wherein information known only to the dead has been conveyed to the living.

The moment anyone begins to wonder about what happens to those who die, he is inevitably led to consider the related phenomena of dream life, for experiences with the dead are precisely similar to some of the experiences of the dream consciousness.

Dream Solutions of Problems

One of the first results of a serious study of dreams is that almost anyone can obtain proof of the fact that we are far more intelligent when we sleep than in waking consciousness. This is shown by the fact that mathematical problems have been solved in dreams, inventions perfected, whole books planned and intricate musical compositions worked out. In many cases the best efforts of the waking brain consciousness have been concentrated unsuccessfully for days on a solution, and then the problem has been clearly and lucidly solved in a dream of a few moments. Robert Louis Stevenson, Lewis Carroll, and many scientists, doctors, teachers, lawyers and inventors testify to this truth. We give one example.

Mathematical Problem Solved

Newton Preston, a teacher of mathematics, always worked out beforehand the problems he planned to present to his class. One day he came across a problem he could not solve. He worked for some days at it and finally appealed to other teachers. They were unable to help him. On the evening before he was to present the problem to his class he worked late into the night but retired without success. In the morning he went to his desk to gather up his papers, and, to his astonishment, he found the whole thing worked out perfectly in his own handwriting. He asked his wife where the paper came from. She told him that he got up in the night and sat for a long time at his desk writing, and then came back to bed. He had done the whole thing in his sleep.

It is not necessary to act as a somnambulist and put material figures on paper—one might have remembered it as a dream. But on the other hand, many people cannot remember dreams clearly. They may have a very clear and vivid experience and be perfectly confident that they will remember it, but it vanishes completely before they reach the breakfast table. The loss can be averted by making a few notes at the moment, not at a later time.

Freedom from the Body

Once we are convinced that we are wiser asleep than awake, the next step is to prove that we can function intelligently when the body is unconscious. Many have been able to prove that. Many have stood outside the body and observed it as a thing apart while undergoing an operation, or when on the verge of dying, from which they recovered, or merely by being projected from the body in sleep.

Out-of-the-Body Experience

An example of consciousness functioning intelligently apart from the physical body is given by Mr. W. Martin of Liverpool, England, in the *Sunday Express* of May 26, 1935. He writes:

"In 1911, at the age of sixteen, I was staying about twelve miles away from my own home when a high wall was blown down by a sudden gust of wind as I was passing. A huge coping stone hit me on top of the head.

"It then seemed as if I could see myself lying on the ground, huddled up, with one corner of the stone resting on my head and quite a number of people rushing toward me. I watched them move the stone and someone took off his coat and put it under my head, and I heard all their comments: 'Fetch a doctor.' 'His neck is broken.' 'Skull smashed.'

"One man then wanted to know if anyone knew where I lived, and on being told that I was lodging just around the corner, he instructed them to carry me there.

"Now all this time it appeared as though I were disembodied from the form lying on the ground and suspended in midair in the center of the group, and I could hear everything that was being said.

"As they started to carry me it was remarked that it would come as a blow to my people, and I was immediately conscious of a desire to be with my mother. Instantly I was at home, and father and mother were just sitting down to their midday meal. On my entrance mother sat bolt upright in her chair and said, 'Bert, something has happened to our boy.'

"There followed an argument, but my mother refused to be pacified, and said that if she caught the 2 p.m. train she could be with me before three.

"She had hardly left the room when there came a knock at the front door. It was a porter from the railway station with a telegram saying that I was badly hurt.

"Then suddenly I was again transported—this time it seemed to be against my wish—to a bedroom, where a woman whom I recognized was in bed, and two other women were quietly bustling around, and a doctor was leaning over the bed. Then the doctor had a baby in his hands. At once I became aware of an almost irresistible impulse to press my face through the back of the baby's head so that my face would come out at the same place as the child's.

"The doctor said, 'It looks as though we had lost them both,' and again I felt the urge to take the baby's place to show him he was wrong, but the thought of my mother crying turned my thoughts in her direction, when straightaway I was in a railway carriage with her and my father.

"I was still with them when they arrived at my lodgings and were shown into the room where I had been put to bed. Mother sat beside the bed and I longed to comfort her, and the realization came that I ought to do the same thing I had felt impelled to do in the case of the baby and climb into the body on the bed.

"At last I succeeded, and the effort caused the real me* to sit up in bed fully conscious. Mother made me lie down again, but I said that I was all right, and remarked that it was odd she knew

---

* Most people believe that the physical body is the "real me" but the real self is the "observer" who, as in this case, was aware of the location of his body and was also aware of the entire experience here related.

something was wrong before the porter had brought the telegram.

"Both she and Dad were amazed at my knowledge. Their astonishment was further increased when I repeated almost word for word some of the conversation they had had at home and in the train. I said that I had been close to birth as well as death, and told them that Mrs. Wilson, who lived close to us at home, had had a baby that day, but it was dead because I would not get into its body. We subsequently learned that Mrs. Wilson died on the same day at 2:05 P.M. after delivering a still-born girl."

That is but one illustration of many thousands which have been recorded. There are those who would dismiss such an account as "imagination." But it would be a greater tax on intelligence to accept such a weak explanation in the face of the minute accuracy of the experience.

Having evidenced that we possess a wider consciousness than that of the body and the brain, and that this higher intelligence can function quite apart from an unconscious body, we are ready to go a step beyond and give evidence of survival after death, when there is no physical body. Here we are faced with a vast amount of evidence, but it is my purpose only to use examples where there is tangible physical proof of authenticity. When evidence is produced which may be seen and handled,

it becomes difficult to dismiss it with words like
"coincidence," "chance," "sex repressions," "imagination" or "delusion."

The Arcadian Travelers

Cicero relates that two Arcadian travelers arrived one day seeking rooms at an inn. But as there
was not sufficient room at the inn, one friend went
to a private house. In the night the man in the private dwelling dreamed that his friend was appeal-
ing to him for help—that he was being attacked. It
awakened him, but vivid though the experience
was he dismissed it as "just a dream." On his falling asleep the friend again came to him astrally
and said: "It's too late—I have been murdered and
they have hidden my body in a cart of manure in a
field." In the morning he went to the inn and found
his friend missing. But his dream had told him exactly where to find the body and he discovered it
precisely as he had dreamed.

There we have information conveyed first from
one living man to another, and secondly, from the
same man, now dead, to a living man.

"I Stole Money"

Mrs. C. D. Diehl of Omaha relates the following
story from her home town in Sweden. A certain
Mrs. Greta Pearson living there became ill and

died. Shortly afterwards Mrs. Pearson was seen as an apparition at various times by numbers of the villagers. She was usually seen in the open between the house and the barn. Mr. Jacob Erickson, an uncle of Mrs. Diehl, never having seen a ghost, was anxious to accost the late Mrs. Pearson and he determined, if successful, to have a chat with the ghost and find out what she wanted. He was successful, and the following conversation took place between the living and the dead.

Mr. Erickson said: "What's the matter with you —don't you know that you are disturbing the whole neighborhood?"

The ghost replied: "Oh, I'm so thankful you spoke to me. I'm Mrs. Greta Pearson who just died."

"Yes," he said, "I know, and you are causing a lot of talk."

She replied: "When I was living I used to steal money from my husband. I kept it hidden in a handkerchief in the barn, and no one knows where to look for it. I can't rest until that money is restored to my husband. If I point out the place will you promise to recover it and return it to him?"

Mr. Erickson gave his word and the ghost pointed out the place. As it was dark and the task required a ladder, Mr. Erickson waited until morning. He then related the incident to the mayor, the postmaster and the doctor of the village, and with these witnesses he recovered the money and restored it to the husband. The husband was completely ignorant of the wife's pilferings and had not missed the money since it had been taken a little at a time. The ghost of Mrs. Greta Pearson, troubled no longer—earthbound no longer—was not seen again.

No one living knew that there was any money in the barn, but a dead woman conveyed to a living man the information that it was there and pointed out its hiding place.

Knowledge vs. Ignorance

Those who have definite knowledge of survival after death are up against a peculiar problem. They are faced by ignorant people who have no such knowledge and who, on the basis of ignorance, deny the evidence and ignore the facts.

In order to gain knowledge on any subject we must begin at the beginning. In the case of this subject no one has any right to even an opinion until he has studied and experimented with the dream consciousness, with telepathy and with clairvoyance. Now that Dr. Alexis Carrel has given public testimony that the fact of clairvoyance is true, lesser men of learning are becoming more courageous about dealing with this subject. We need not, therefore, pay much attention to those who ignore the facts and deny the evidence. On the other hand, not all the evidence is authentic, and conclusions drawn from such evidence are not necessarily correct.

Mind-Reading

As an illustration of this, we relate the following experience of Mr. J. W. Brodie-Innes. He relates in *The Occult Review* that he went to a woman who called herself a "Lady Inspirationist." She insisted with all visitors that she did not want to know their names or anything about them. To one man after a silence of three or four minutes she began: "You have a strange and romantic career ———" and then for twenty minutes told a story of wild romance and adventure. She stopped, looked him full in the face and asked: "Is that correct?" He said, "Perfectly, but it's not me." "What do you mean?" she asked. He replied: "You have told me almost line for line a story I am writing, which is not yet finished and which no one has seen. It is locked up in my desk." She explained: "I saw it. Every incident passed before me as if it were your memory of your own life."

What the "Lady Inspirationist" did was to exercise telepathy and read the mind of an author who had created characters out of his imagination, and she was ready to accept these fictions as living people.

There is a wealth of literature on the subject of survival after death, and those interested are obligated to study it before too dogmatically expressing opinions. The true scientific attitude of mind is that of the agnostic, who says "I do not know," as against the gnostic, or one who does know. But knowledge in this field, as in all other departments of life, is ever expanding, and no one knows everything about it. The important thing is to maintain an open attitude of mind.

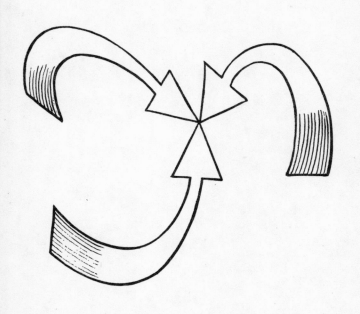

Make me always ready to come to you with clean hands and straight eyes. So when life fades, as the fading sunset, my spirit may come to you without shame.

An Indian Prayer

2

THE ONLY THREE WAYS OF DYING

Many people fear death. We fear only that which we do not understand. A man can be frightened only if he is ignorant. When he knows what to expect he can anticipate an event and meet it fearlessly.

The first step is an application of common sense and knowledge. There are only three ways in which a man can die, and by knowing what sensations to expect, fear may be removed, and the process of transition may be rendered interesting if not delightful. The actual transition in all three methods is physically painless, whatever pains may be endured leading up to transition. Maeterlinck says, "Illnesses have nothing in common with that which ends them. They form part of life not of death."*

Syncope

The first way in which death may come is called Syncope. That word means "to cut short." We have "syncopation" in music. Death caused by syncope is always sudden, as when one is struck

---

* Maurice Maeterlinck, *Death* (London: Methuen & Co., Ltd., 1911), pp. 10–11.

unconscious by lightning, or by being hit with an iron girder, or by being knocked out in an automobile accident or a prize fight. Indeed, "knocked out" is a true description, for the person is literally thrown out of his body. Anyone who has ever fainted, or been rendered unconscious (on the operating table or in any other way) knows exactly how it feels to die through syncope.

Sometimes, in syncope, there is a slight anticipation of death, as in the case of a blood clot. A man may feel it coming just in time to say: "Everything is going black," and he has hardly finished speaking when all is over. But that is no different from the sensation immediately preceding fainting. Syncope, then, is one way to die and no one need fear it.

Asphyxiation

The second method of dying is through asphyxiation. That means suffocation or without pulsation. Hereward Carrington describes it as "loss of consciousness because of imperfect oxidation of the blood." We cannot live without air. Drowning cuts off air, but drowning is universally proclaimed to be a pleasant sensation, according to those who have experienced it. The physiological description of drowning is no doubt substantially true of all forms of asphyxiation. There is just a deep respiration by which the bubbles of air are expelled from the lungs. Then there is an effort to draw in air, but the effort is ineffectual because the muscles are engaged in keeping water out. The attempts to breathe are repeated several times and with each attempt a small quantity of air is expelled in the form of bubbles. When the air cells are completely empty the person becomes unconscious, the muscles relax and only then does water flow into the lungs. The process is much quicker than asphyxiation by gas because gas usually contains a small quantity of oxygen also.

Persons revived by the pulmotor have a feeling that they are being pulled back into their bodies by a rope which they cannot resist, although they often ardently desire to resist.

When oxygen is cut off by gas, carbon-monoxide, or water, death begins at the lungs and almost immediately paralyzes the muscles of the body. Nearly everyone has experienced a graphic illustration of death through asphyxia if he has attended a crowded meeting in a small room not properly ventilated. Everyone begins to get sleepy. In this case, however, the muscles are relaxed. But open a window and start a cool breeze of clean air over the crowd, and they all wake up. The policeman directing traffic at a crowded intersection becomes half drugged at the end of a day due to partial asphyxiation.

We may say that death through asphyxiation is

quite painless if the process is gradual but that the preliminaries are painful under acute conditions. In acute cases, death is mercifully quick as in syncope. It not infrequently happens that a person is found peacefully dead in a small room in which a gas stove has failed on a cold morning. But this gradual and painless sleep of death is different from the painful but quick struggle in acute cases preceding asphyxiation while the patient is gasping for air, and may be "blue in the face" in the struggle. But the moment the struggle ceases, or even subsides, all pain ceases. This is due to the natural anesthetic or loss of feeling resulting from carbon-dioxide's being deposited in the lungs, which cannot throw it off. Nature therefore sees to it that death from asphyxiation, both gradual and acute, is perfectly painless when it comes to transition.

Breakdown of Vital Organs or Function

The third method of dying is by the breaking down of some vital organ, which then gradually extends its death-dealing sway over other organs until finally the heart ceases to beat and the lungs to breathe. This process is much more gradual than we usually suppose. Hereward Carrington says: "Ninety-five percent of civilized adults are now stricken with fatal diseases—no bodily organ can perish from disease in less than ten years—usually it requires twenty years."

The vital organ or function that first fails will be the weakest organ of the body—made weakest by illness contracted perhaps years previously. That varies with each individual. If a man has a good sound, balanced body, with all vital organs equally strong, the first one to fail is usually the liver. One by one the others follow. A dying person, when far enough along, does not cry; not because he lacks feeling, but because the tear glands have ceased to function.

Every person should know which is the weakest organ of his body, and he should follow through a definite program to cleanse that weak organ of poisons. Avoid drugs. The blood stream, which carries nourishment to the organs, and carries away sewage, should not be diluted with nicotine and alcohol but fed with life-giving elements. Carbon-dioxide is burned and gotten rid of by deep breathing; few people, however, know how to breathe properly. The handicaps we create to avoid health are indeed fearful and wonderful.

But whatever the first organ or function to break down, the poisons of broken down tissue gradually circulate and bring about ultimate death. The death rattle is caused by fluids accumulating in the windpipe as the air passes through. It sounds unpleasant but at that stage there is almost no pain.

So long as there is vigorous life in various organs of the body, they combine instinctively to sustain life. They tend to succumb reluctantly but have to submit one after another. So long as there is resistance there is pain, but immediately one relaxes to die, pain ceases because waste tissue acts as an anesthetic. In some cases there are convulsive movements as the body attempts to adjust itself to the expulsion of accumulating poisons; and expressions of pain flit across the features and heavy breathing is observed. These are internal adjustments corresponding to a rearrangement of pillows and bedclothes to make a patient comfortable.

Under this third method of dying by the breaking down of functions and organs no two persons experience the same sensations.

Death is a physiological process like breathing, laughing, or crying and should be just as painless. William Hunter, the celebrated surgeon, said as he died: "If I had the strength to hold a pen I would tell how easy and delightful it is to die."

These, then, are the three ways of dying, syncope, or sudden death; failure of respiration, or asphyxiation; and the failure of bodily functions.

There should be specialists who do nothing but devise ways and means of easing the painful preliminaries of transition. We have the oxygen tent and other means but they are available only to a few people. Nature takes care that the actual transition is painless.

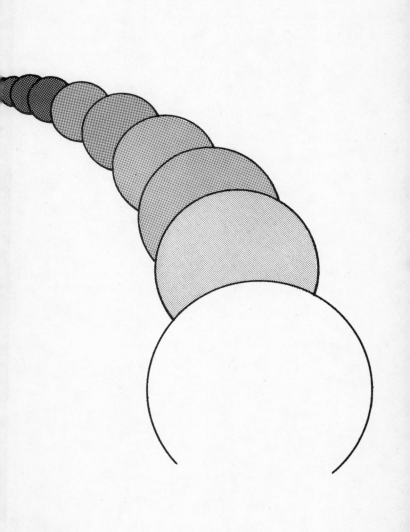

I think there are many reasons for this flight away from facing death calmly. One of the most important facts is that dying nowadays is more gruesome in many ways, namely, more lonely, mechanical, and dehumanized; at times, it is even difficult to determine technically when the time of death has occurred.

Dying becomes lonely and impersonal because the patient is often taken out of his familiar environment and rushed to an emergency room.

Elisabeth Kubler-Ross, *On Death and Dying*
(N.Y.: Macmillan Publishing Co., 1974).

3

THE PROCESS OF "DYING"

It is not necessary to describe the process of sudden death because it is all over so quickly. The most descriptive illustration is to liken it to fainting, as explained in our previous chapter.

The other two ways of dying—by failure of respiration or by failure of a vital organ—may be rapid or slow. If by asphyxiation, or failure of respiration—in other words, by suffocation, it is a fairly quick death like drowning—the sensation of pain ceases the moment one gives up the struggle and relaxes. It is then said to be very pleasant, as in freezing to death, according to the testimony of those who have inadvertently tried it. But if the failure of respiration is a slow process, there is even less pain, due to the fact that as the carbondioxide increases it acts as a partial, and later as a complete anesthetic. A person unable to breathe properly becomes very tired and weak and must be handled gently.

When one is dying due to the breakdown of a vital organ, there is also pain appropriate to the particular disease so long as that organ or function struggles to survive, but when the process of dying begins, the pain gradually becomes less and finally ceases. Sometimes it ceases suddenly as in the case of a ruptured appendix. But lack of pain does not mean that the disease has vanished. The blood circulation, carrying poisons all over the body, may tend to increase pain at first but soon that blood stream, like the lungs laden with carbon-dioxide, makes a man insensible to pain. He may sink into a coma, which is a sleep of unconsciousness; or, he may remain awake until the last moment. There are so many complications in dying that no two processes will be alike.

The people who take longest to die are those who imagine that the physical world and the physical body are the be-all and end-all of life. One who has been materialistic all his or her life, very much centered on the body and material possessions, may say when dying at the age of—say eighty or more—"I wish I could go—why can't I die and have done with it?" For a material minded person it is an unreasonable request. Why should anyone expect to overcome the thought habits of a lifetime by a mere wish when one is in a tight spot? If, on the other hand, one has always regarded death as a mere incident, like sleep, it is easy to relax and let go. The best way is just to go to sleep and not wake up again. Many people do that. We have all gone to sleep many times and no one thinks it very serious or anything to be afraid of. When we fall asleep we leave the body through the center at the top of the head, but the silver cord remains unbroken. We shall discuss that silver cord in detail later. In an ancient liturgy the anointing with holy oil in baptism was called "cleansing the gateway of the soul." It is the natural exit. But disease sometimes causes a person to try to leave in an unnatural way—perhaps through the mouth, or the side, or the solar plexus. Sometimes psychic practices upset the natural process.

Assuming that it is to be a normal transition, the person may observe that the five senses fail in the reverse order in which they were acquired during the long evolutionary process. The first sense to be developed was touch. Next we developed hearing. A mineral can "hear" as is seen by a glass shattered by a violin note. The next sense developed was sight, then taste and finally smell. There are, of course, still two more senses to be developed, and some already partially possess the sixth sense of clairvoyance and clairaudience. Anyone who has a feeling of sensitiveness is exercising the sixth sense to some degree. As these senses leave, or become insensitive, those remaining become more acute. Therefore, quiet must be maintained. The hands and feet become cold because the blood circulation is becoming slower. Livingstone's last words were: "It's getting cold; put more grass on the hut." But the cold was in his body.

As the life forces withdraw towards the heart one suddenly remembers having done all this before in former lives on earth, and that memory banishes whatever apprehension a person may have. The peaceful countenance of the dead testifies to that. It not infrequently happens that the candidate for death will see some of his dead relatives and friends, as well as angels. For angels do attend and help at both birth and death. When the Reverend Dwight L. Moody was dying, he said: "Earth is dissolved; heaven opens before me—do not call me back. If this is death, it is beautiful. Dwight! Irene! I see the children!"

As the life forces withdraw further there is a tingling sensation, like the flow of blood into a foot that has been "asleep"; this relaxing sensation is due to a slow breaking of etheric threads as the etheric matter of the body disengages itself from the numerous nerve threads. It is not painful, but gives a sense of relaxation. Slowly one falls asleep and when he is asleep he is "dead." There is certainly nothing to fear in any part of the process of dying.

Some people do not take so long; they quit the body suddenly. The transition may be likened to the opening of ripe fruit where, for example, the stone of a peach comes clean away from the fruit without clinging. It is all over in a moment. In other cases it is no different from falling asleep.

The next immediate sensation varies with the individual. Some remain unconscious—anywhere from a few hours to a few days or even weeks in the case of a person who firmly believes death means annihilation of consciousness. But all wake up after awhile and begin the process of adjustment to the new conditions. Many are immediately awake the minute they are dead—far more awake than they ever were in physical life.

We Are the Dead

It is we in the physical world who are really the dead because we are in a world of only three dimensions. St. Paul says to us, supposedly alive, "Awake, thou that sleepest and arise from the dead." It is clear that St. Paul considered the physical waking consciousness not merely a sleep form of life, but a form of death. And St. John in the Revelations says to people on earth: "You have the name of being alive, but you are dead." Do not feel insulted; it means, as Virgil asserted: "Souls are deadened by earthly forms" and, as Plotinus declared: "Death to the soul is to descend into matter and be entirely subjected to it." The chief function of religion is to point to a life and consciousness wider than that of "this body of death," as St. Paul called the physical body, but few people heed the call to a more abundant life.

Transition Is Pleasant

The immediate sensation of many as they get free from the body, and this is vividly true in the case of one who has been suffering great pain, is that an instantaneous cure has taken place. One moment there is pain; the next is one of complete relief from pain. The impression is a delightful feeling of lightness and buoyancy. The airy feeling is due to the fact that physical gravity, which gives the sensation of weight, loses its power as soon as man is free from his body. It is the same feeling we experience in dreams of flying, drifting or floating. If one has a dream of being out of the body and tries to resist being drawn back into it, he will find that his feet and body become heavy. But when the silver cord is broken that tired, weary and heavy feeling disappears.

There is so much to be said about the silver cord that we will keep that for a separate chapter, but it really belongs to the process of dying, preceding transition. There is also another important event that precedes transition called the review of life, to which we will devote more detailed study.

There is really nothing to be afraid of in the process of dying; physical pain can be reduced and alleviated by science and loving thoughtfulness, and the actual transition is a satisfying and quite pleasing experience. We will give just one example out of many testimonies. This we take from the *Atlantic Monthly*, January, 1930.

How It May Feel to Die

Dorothy McL . . . . . . all but died after a surgical operation. The watching nurses and her sister had not thought she could survive the night; and she herself had been clearly conscious that she was dying. She said it was the most heart-satisfying experience she had ever known, and that at first she gave herself up altogether to the profound pleasure she was feeling. But gradually she began to be troubled by her sister's grief and for her sake made a monstrous effort at recovery; it succeeded and she re-entered mortal life. "But I was convinced," she said, "that I was making an enormous sacrifice; I thought so at the time, and now, when years have gone by, I think so still."

I have been warned that if I make dying too attractive, people might play with the idea of suicide. But suicide is exceedingly unpleasant and solves no problems. It only makes matters much worse, as we shall see when we discuss what happens to suicides and what being earthbound involves.

It has also been suggested that if we make the wider life so much more powerful and attractive than earth life, many may become dissatisfied with the earth and become drifters. There is no such danger for one who knows the purpose of this physical world and the great value of a physical body.

It is the secret of the world that all things subsist and do not die, but only retire a little from sight and afterwards return again. . . . Nothing is dead; men feign themselves dead, and endure mock funerals and mournful Obituaries, and there they stand looking out of the window, sound and well, in some new and strange disguise. Jesus is not dead; he is very well alive: nor John, nor Paul, nor Mahomet, nor Aristotle; at times we believe we have seen them all, and could easily tell the names under which they go.

Ralph Waldo Emerson, *Nominalist and Realist*

4

THE PHYSIOLOGICAL
PAINLESSNESS OF DEATH

Lord Bacon said: "It is as natural to die as to be born." Nature evidently intended that the end of man should be as painless as his beginning. At birth, the infant does not receive conscious impressions yet he cries and kicks by muscular reaction; so it is with death so far as muscular reaction is concerned. The so-called "death agony," "the last struggle," "the pangs of death" are erroneous if associated with pain; they are largely unconscious muscular reactions. Professor J. Cook Wilson in the *London Times* described the terrible respiratory struggles of his father when dying from cardiac failure supervening on influenza. The harrowing struggles of the dying man were apparently so painful that his son could hardly believe the assurance of medical attendants that the patient knew nothing of them. After several hours passed, apparently in intense agony, the patient woke and volunteered the statement that he had spent a comfortable night.

We are not speaking of the days and weeks preceding death but of the actual transition. There is often much pain in connection with the preliminaries, especially when one is resisting the process

of transition, but after all, those pains are but a
continuation of what man has been more or less
accustomed to. He is fairly familiar with that suffering and can stand it, and modify it and relieve
it.*

Death is necessary to life, for without death we
could not live. Cell tissue breaks down every
minute and the waste is excreted through the
lungs, skin and excretory organs. That is why internal and external cleanliness is necessary.

We need not dwell on the painlessness of death
by syncope or by asphyxiation for we discussed
that in our last chapter, but it is well to explain
why the slower methods of dying are also quite
painless when the transition takes place. In the col-
lapse of vital functions and vital organs, and when
the broken down cell tissues invades other parts of
the body, a condition called *coma* intervenes.

Coma is a state of unconsciousness resembling
sleep, It may last for days. It is well to understand
this condition of coma because in a modified form
it precedes the transition of many people. As the
end of life draws near, the respirations become
slow and shallow, interrupted now and then by a
deep sighing inspiration as though the lungs were

---

* Gerald Heard defines pain as excess energy crying out for release.
We feel no pain when our minds are otherwise occupied. Gerald
Heard, *Pain, Sex and Time*.

vainly endeavoring to throw off the weakness that is creeping over them. At the same time the blood becomes saturated with carbonic acid gas. Also at the same time the heart valves can only propel the blood a short distance through its arterial channels, thus causing the extremities to grow cold. The blood that does reach the brain is not only small in quantity but is laden with stupifying carbonic gas (the same deadly fumes formed from burning charcoal) and this destroys both consciousness and sensation. The face may be cold, the lips purple due to lack of circulation; cold perspiration (death damp) collects upon the brow, but as the power of receiving impressions is gone there can be no sensation of pain. If there are convulsive muscular movements they are automatic.

In cases where the senses are retained to the last, the mind is usually calm and collected and the body free from pain. There is suffering from disease, but transition itself is always a relief. It is not uncommon for the dying, after lying in a semiconscious condition for hours, to start up suddenly with glowing face, point eagerly at some object or person in the invisible world and with animated words describe what they so clearly see; and then relax and fall backward dead.

If that happens with someone you are attending do not be startled or disturbed—be sympathetic and encouraging—support the half reclining form in its temporary strength. It is also not uncommon for one in a coma to return to the body at times and be conscious of those around the bed; then the body sinks to sleep again and the patient may look upon it as a worn out garment. In later visits to his body he finds he has less control of the senses, especially those of sight and taste.

In death resulting from a slowing up of the blood circulation there is sometimes a swelling of the veins that looks distressing, but again there is not as much pain as there seems to be. This swelling is due to certain gases confined in the blood stream which separate and form a pneumatosis or swelling of the veins.

Evidence of Painlessness

As further evidence of the painlessness of death and so-called death struggles, physicians interested in the subject have asked people who have just gone through the most fearful looking contortions and twistings of features: "Tell me, what were your sensations a moment ago?" And the patient replied: "Why, I have just awakened from a refreshing sleep."

Dr. Robert McKenna tells that one of the worst cases of eclamptic convulsions he ever saw occurred in a woman of twenty-eight. "I was present," he said, "at the onset and saw agony graven in sharp characters upon the sufferer's face. But when the convulsion was over, the patient slowly recovered consciousness and, as she opened her eyes, said: 'I have just had a nice sleep.' "

We have ample evidence that those who are knocked out feel nothing. A priest was rendered unconscious in an automobile accident in which his companion was instantly killed. He said that he found himself standing in the road by the car, looking down on his unconscious body but he felt no pain. This testimony of living witnesses could be multiplied many times over. Further evidence is given by people who are actually killed, but not everyone is willing to accept such evidence because it depends on clairvoyance. We therefore give only one example. One soldier said: "I was quite suddenly shot out of my body and felt no pain whatever. . . . I simply folded my arms, had a good look at my body, and thought: 'Is that all?' I could not wrench myself away immediately from my body, because it was not quite dead, and I accompanied it when the stretcher bearers carried it to the dressing rooms. But I felt no pain." He then said that he lost consciousness—in other words, died. The British Medical Journal says: "The moment immediately preceding death from disease is that of utter insensibility to all pain, or of a delightful passivity, from the universal relaxation of everything which pertains to the physical condition."

Dr. Jerome Anderson of San Francisco once

asked an intelligent young man who was dying how he felt, since they were both interested in the sensation of dying; the young man replied: "I feel as though I am about to faint." The next moment he did "faint"—that is, he died.

Many famous people, whose word we can trust, have given testimony as to the painlessness of death, just at the moment they passed away. At such a time there is every reason to believe that they are telling the truth for there is no object in doing anything else, added to the fact of their life-long reputations for truth and honesty. Stonewall Jackson who was in a coma for some days, due to gangrene, supposed to be most painful, awakened out of his coma and said: "Let us cross over the river, and rest in the shade of those trees." Thomas Edison, also awakening out of a coma, said: "It is very beautiful over there." The last words of the great German poet Schiller were: "Many things are growing plain and clear to my understanding." Daniel Webster said: "I still live." Louis XIV expressed surprise that dying was so easy, contrary to everything he had been led to expect. He said: "I thought dying had been more difficult." Goethe's last words were: "Light, more light!" Beethoven, who was deaf, said: "I shall hear!"

There is no pain in dying. From the physical point of view it is like the ebbing of a tide, a receding wave, a relaxation. But from the point of view of life beyond, it is like the passing of twilight into the dawn of sunrise. If you have inhaled the perfume of a flower but have never seen one; if you have dreamed a dream of loveliness but never have seen it embodied; if you have thought of love but never loved, then you can imagine what earth life is, compared to life beyond the earth. The first great wonder is that everything in material life remains the same, but is transfigured, for here we see only the shadow of reality. If we look at a tray of minerals they look dull and earthy, but look at them under ultra violet light and they shine like precious stones and take on life. Is it so fanciful, then, for St. John and other Christian clairvoyants to speak of crystal, gold and rainbow colors? They are not materializing the invisible world, but stating facts that advancing science is beginning to prove.

"When the higher vehicles have left the dense body they are still connected with it by a slender, glistening, silvery Cord, shaped much like two figure sixes reversed, one upright and one horizontally placed, the two connected at the extremeties of the hooks. One is fastened to the heart by means of the seed atom, and it is the rupture of the seed atom which causes the heart to stop. The Cord itself is not snapped until the panorama of the past life, contained in the vital body, has been reviewed. . . . The Silver Cord snaps at the point where the "sixes" unite, half remaining with the dense body (and etheric double) and half with the higher vehicles. From the time the Cord snaps the dense body is quite "dead." The rupture (of the seed atom in the heart) releases the vital body, and that, together with the desire body and mind, floats above the visible body for not more than three and one-half days, while the Spirit is engaged in reviewing the past life." These pictures are in the Light and Reflecting Ethers which are attached to the heart seed atom, and it is this stuff (ethers) which is etched into the desire body during the panoramic review.

Max Heindel, *The Silver Cord and The Seed Atoms* (Oceanside, Calif.: Rosicrucian Fellowship).

5

THE SILVER CORD

In the Book of Ecclesiastes 12:6 there is a reference to the silver cord in these words: "or ever the silver cord be loosed or the golden bowl be broken." An enormous number of nerve threads come together at the base of the brain and are then interwoven throughout the matter of the brain itself. Thus we may regard the brain as a switchboard controlling the telegraph system of nerves and muscles of the body and the brain in turn, as operating through the trunk line of the silver cord by the higher consciousness. The silver cord gathers the nerve threads terminating in the brain into an etheric cable which is attached to the suture at the top of the head, called in Sanskrit the *brahmarandra* center, or the aperture of *Brahma*. It is through this center at the crown of the head that the consciousness normally departs from the human body, partially in sleep or meditation, and completely at death.

An ancient Christian Liturgy[1] speaks of the anointing of that center with the sacred Chrism[2] in

---

[1] Sacrament of Baptism, Liberal Catholic Liturgy, which is based on an early Greek Orthodox source.
[2] Consecrated oil for anointing.

Baptism as "cleansing the gateway of the soul." This silver cord is constructed of etheric matter, finer than any physical atmosphere or gases, yet it is nevertheless physical matter. It may be likened to the umbilical cord and it is the connecting link between the physical and the astral body which St. Paul calls the spiritual body. So long as the silver cord remains intact life can be maintained in the body, but the moment it is loosed or severed, death ensues immediately and there is no coming back.

The silver cord is capable of almost infinite extension so that a person can, in sleep, travel miles away from his physical body and yet keep it alive. Most people do not go far from their bodies during sleep but hover near like watch dogs. If one attempted to draw them away from their brown study or introspection they would immediately fly back to the body, and awake with palpitating heart, because they would mistakenly fear that to go far away from the body would mean its death.

In order to get some conception of the silver cord, we ought to have some general knowledge of the nervous system. If we look at a diagram of the nervous system in a medical book, it will be observed that these nerve threads extend all over the body; some are bundled together, many have sub-branches, all of them have their specific function and they all perform their duty without confusion.

These innumerable nerve filaments come together at the top of the spine and are diffused through the brain. The silver cord extends into the invisible world from the crown of the head.

Imagine a cable of many hundreds of slender nerve threads, each having a clearly defined line of etheric matter extending from it where it joins the body, but becoming more ethereal as it penetrates into the finer ethers until it becomes very tenuous. A good illustration is a radio beam thrown out miles into the ether and along which an airplane may be guided accurately and safely, just as in the children's stories the fairy slides down a moonbeam. And just as we have innumerable wavelengths on our radio and the symphony is but a fraction of an inch away from a news broadcast, yet they never intrude upon one another. So in like manner the silver cord of one person never gets entangled with that of another, because each person is unique, just as no two leaves of a tree are exactly alike, or no two thumb prints match.

During life the higher consciousness controls and directs the physical body through an etheric telegraph system. The silver cord does not transmit vitality to the body. Vitality pours into the body from the sun and is absorbed by the spleen, and it is there split up into seven streams of force and directed along the nerve fibers to the various etheric centers. No doubt a certain amount of energy flows through the silver cord along with the consciousness, as we shall see in a moment when we come to break it in death, but the vitality that sustains the body in health is absorbed mainly through the spleen.

In sleep, especially with a person who is afraid to go far from his body, the silver cord has the appearance of being an umbilical cord except that it is connected at the brain center and not at the navel. It appears almost tangible. But if one travels some distance from the body it would be more comparable to a radio beam.

Having described briefly the silver cord, we will now observe what happens in dying, and how the cord is severed in death. For the sake of convenience of study we will allow our hypothetical candidate about two and a half hours in which to die. This description is a composite one and a condensation of studies by a number of independent investigators who have observed the process.

In discussing the process of dying, we explained that as weakness creeps over the body and the breathing becomes labored and the heart action weak, the extremities get cold due to slower blood circulation. While this is taking place the vital organs appear to resist the withdrawal of vital force because they instinctively feel it means the end of them. But the instinctive clinging of the vital organs to the sustaining energy flowing along the nerve filaments is only a momentary internal struggle. As the vitality is withdrawn it is gathered together from the sacral plexus, the solar plexus, the spleen and the throat into the heart and the brain. The brain becomes highly charged with life forces, with *prana* and vitality, ten times more so than it ever was in the best of health.

The Golden Bowl

As the rest of the body becomes negative and dead, the heart and brain become more alive because all the forces of the body are now concentrated in the upper part of it. When a dying person says: "Everything is becoming clear; my mind is more lucid than it has ever been," we may know that transition is taking place. The head becomes intensely brilliant; it is like a golden bowl. All this time the silver cord also becomes more alive; etheric matter flows over it like a rapidly moving fluorescent light, but imperceptibly extracting the life force more and more somewhat as a suction. Where the silver cord joins the main nerve ganglia it consists of thousands of very fine threads. As the life forces flow back into the higher world, these threads begin to break. As they break, the ends curl up like the raveling of a silk thread. The actual transition comes when the link between the heart and the brain blows out like a fuse, and then the final threads of the silver cord break as the golden bowl is broken. A very small quantity of etheric matter flows back into the dead physical body and is diffused over that body along the nervous system. This afterwards evaporates, as it were, into the surrounding ether. It is probable that the length of time that a body remains in a state of preservation would depend on the amount of diffused remnant of vitality. It is therefore best to allow the body to remain undisturbed for some hours.

The Atomic Web

Just as an unborn child is enclosed in the protecting membrane of the placenta, to which is attached the umbilical cord, which is severed at birth, so during life the body is enclosed in a protecting web of atomic matter, to which is attached the silver cord, which is severed at death. The silver cord, before it is severed, draws all of this protecting placenta together and gently absorbs or ingests it, and the moment after it is withdrawn through the silver cord then it is that the silver cord is severed. The parallel is almost perfect, for while the unborn child is safe so long as the placenta remains intact, any rupture would cause a dangerous dry birth. So also any rupture of the atomic web during life causes a great loss of vitality, as well as opens one up prematurely to psychic influences. This etheric atomic web may be injured by alcohol, narcotics, excessive use of tobacco, tea, coffee and drugs; also by unwise psychic practices.

What happens then is that the volatile constituents rush out of the protecting sheath in a direction opposite to that intended by nature, tearing the web in much the same way that the insulation is burnt from an electric wire. It is for this reason that Holy Oil is used in the Church when anointing the centers prescribed in the Healing Service.

The reader may recall that we stated in a previous chapter that some people try to leave the body in abnormal ways—through the solar plexus, the side, or the neck, instead of through the center at the top of the head. The normal outlet for consciousness is via the silver cord.

Extreme Unction

If the departing person is fortunate enough to secure the help of Extreme Unction, the process of dying may be made much more precise and correct as well as more comfortable. Time and again we have had evidence of the efficacy of Extreme Unction, but few people make use of it. It is administered with two ideas in mind; either to effect a healing, usually an almost instantaneous one, or else to assist the person to get out of his body easily.

We will give one instance of almost instantaneous healing by Extreme Unction. I was called to attend a medical doctor in Washington, D.C., obviously dying, or so it seemed, of double pneumonia. He was an old gray-haired man. Two doctors were attending him and he himself knew what to do and what to expect. He looked so far gone that I gave him Extreme Unction in order to help him die easily. I returned to New York and went back to Washington in two weeks and met my doctor friend on the street perfectly well. He said that within twenty-four hours after the Unction was administered he completely cleared his lungs and rapidly recovered.

The anointing of the seven centers of the body governing the vital organs has the effect of assisting in the withdrawal of the vitality from those vital organs to the heart and brain centers, in preparation for the withdrawal of all forces along the cable of the silver cord.

The Absolution of the Dead, which is given as soon after transition as possible, has the effect of making certain that the silver cord *is* severed and all etheric matter *is* withdrawn from the body. It could be cremated almost immediately if desirable. If one cannot have the Extreme Unction, then it is a good plan to cleanse the room with holy water and place a lighted candle at the head and foot of the bed after transition has taken place. These measures act as a protection for the abandoned body so that it will not be disturbed from the other side, and it also protects it from its owner in case he or she is so materialistic as to wish to climb back into it.

It is much the best from all points of view to cremate the body. It is cleaner and more wholesome and it absolutely prevents any misuse of the abandoned body.

The silver cord is not a permanent part of either the physical body or the higher nature. It is nothing more than a bridge of communication—a kind of trans-other-world-cable, and once the body is gone, it has no reason for existence and ceases to be.

There is no death, there is eternal life. I was always convinced of this, but could never clearly formulate my belief. It was based on the fact that life must otherwise be a crying absurdity. . . . If matter is indestructible, why should consciousness disappear forever? . . . Now I saw, by my own experience, that consciousness does not die, that I never ceased, and probably never shall cease, to live.

A. Aputkin (1849—1893), *From Death to Life*

6

THE LIFE IN REVIEW

Everyone is familiar with the testimony of drowning persons that all events of their life pass before them in review in a moment of time. But this review of life is not peculiar to drowning people; it is common to all who die and to many who almost touch death. The editor of a mining newspaper in Butte related that when he was a boy of nine he climbed into an apple tree and fell from a branch to the ground. We all know that the average apple tree is not very tall. Yet in that short fall every incident of his nine years flashed before his mind's eye.

Often this review of life comes in reverse order, beginning with the moment of transition and going back to childhood and infancy. While it takes only an instant, it is advisable to be as quiet as possible around a dying person so that he will not be disturbed. The quiet is needed because, while it is true that the review is almost instantaneous, there is a preparation for it, just as a cessation of thought precedes a flash of genius.

There is no emotion or feeling about the review of life. One surveys it impartially. There are some things about which we may be proud and there are no doubt some things of which we are ashamed, but in the review of life at death we do not feel elated or debased; we look back upon it impersonally as though we stood aside observing ourselves in a philosophical attitude of mind.

An Eagle-Eye View

There is an event, very much like this review of life, that occurs before we are born where we get a rapid glimpse of the incarnation we are about to take. That glimpse occurs in the heaven world at the moment we complete our heaven life and decide to return to earth in a new baby body. We then determine on the main outline of what we plan to do on earth. One of the regrets of life after death is the comparison of our original plan for our life with the actual achievements. It never does come up to par, because *when we are in the timeless and spaceless world* we feel ourselves to be veritable spiritual giants, as indeed we are in that free realm.

We do not realize, and can hardly imagine, the restrictions of time and space. We can readily see that chronological time *is* annihilated when we are able to review in minute detail sixty years of life in a flash of time. Sometimes, as a result of his retrospect, a person may see some things that he could so easily have done differently, that he is ardent to get back into his body to correct them then and there, but it is too late, the body is too far gone. He may look at the body as one sometimes sees it in a mirror and wonders if that can be himself—so like and yet so poor in comparison to the radiant astral body now freed from bondage to the physical.

Those mistakes made in the body can be corrected in the next life on earth, and part of the work between lives is to generate enough determination to correct errors of the past. That determination shows itself in a larger character and a more responsive conscience in a new incarnation. It is wise to attend to the voice of conscience because it is the voice of the higher self who knows our particular plan of life. The reason we plan out our life on earth in specialized sections is because the limitations of the body, of time and space compel limitations. Thus one person specializes in music, another goes into industry, another into education, another is a soldier, sailor, aviator, or housewife and mother. We cannot get all of the wealth of earthly experience that is available to us in one brief life on earth; yet the purpose in coming to earth is "to overcome the world" and to express on earth "the fulness of the Godhead bodily" by becoming "perfect as the Father in heaven is perfect"—our own inmost self. The earth is a rudimentary state of existence, a place to learn primary lessons, because its limitations are not present in life after death.

Basis of Heaven-Life

This swift examination of the tablets of memory when dying is afterwards elaborated to the nth degree, and forms the basis for the process of assimilation of experience into character and conscience, so that when we return to earth we inevitably return with greater wisdom and with an enhanced character. That is the treasure in heaven which neither rust nor moth can corrupt and where thieves cannot break through or steal. Character and wisdom is all we need to conquer the world or to succeed in any walk of life. Thus an ancient Eastern Scripture says: "All actions in their entirety culminate in wisdom." The best way to evolve rapidly is to extract wisdom from experience as we go along day by day, and not wait until after death to do it, possibly with regrets.

The recall of the unforgotten events of life occurs even in sudden death. One man, thrown down a rocky bank twenty feet in a sleeping coach of a railway train, and expecting instant death, experienced between the brink and the bottom, a review of the whole panorama of his life, all the chambers of his memory and conscience illuminated as if a torch had suddenly been lighted inside the brain. In one instant the record of one's whole career on earth is redeemed from oblivion and revealed to oneself. It is a purely private and personal affair. There are no witnesses and it is no last judgment; it is simply a fact in nature.

How is the review of life elaborated? The length

of time spent between lives will be measured according to the wealth of experience gathered during earth life. A primitive man who has very little mental life, or indeed little emotional life, but is absorbed in physical sensation, may have as little as twenty-five years between incarnations. A man like Plato, capable of much abstract thought, is said to have as much as ten thousand years between lives on earth.

How Capacity Is Built

Mr. E. L. Gardner, in an illuminating booklet on THIS WORLD AND THE NEXT gives an illustration of how the review of life is elaborated. Suppose a man has been an ardent book lover all his life. His idea of bliss would be the use of an inexhaustible library. Access to such a library would be easy in the invisible world, and long periods of happy interest are spent among books. Gradually, as the mind becomes more refined, the tendency would be to read philosophy and poetry of the more abstruse character. At a certain height of refinement interest begins to wane and an inner urge for more concrete contacts arises. At that point the heaven world has yielded all that can be assimilated and the man seeks physical experience again because only by restriction do things become concrete and lucid in contrast to the wider but more diffused types of experience. Thus we get some understanding of how the review of life is exhausted.

A person whose main interest in life is diet reform would, after death, delve into the heart of dietetics, and on being reincarnated might become an authority on vitamins and health.

Another may have as his chief absorbing interest the mysteries of radio or television and by following that study would be reborn with natural bent for invention along that line. The same thing is true of doctors and musicians, mechanics and poets. They say: "The idea flashed into my mind," as though it came from nowhere. But it is really knowledge coming from the higher self of that person, from the treasure he has laid up in heaven between lives. There is a practical reason why the Church urges purity of thought, exaltation of feeling and clean diet—it makes "the body of death," as St. Paul calls the physical body, more sensitive to lofty ideas.

When we have digested all our experience, we then take our first step towards reincarnation, and at that stage we cast our mind's eye over our next plan of life. Who determines what that shall be? We do. For each man is the master of his own destiny, however unsatisfactory that destiny may be. It is much like reaching a swift decision to take a six-year course in college. It takes only a moment to make the actual decision, but we have selected our destiny for at least six years.

The Insane

Another point should be recorded, namely, that no one ever dies insane. There is a moment of complete lucidity before even the hopelessly insane pass away. Most people who are insane in the body are completely sane when they are free from it. A friend related an incident that confirmed this statement. She and her family arrived late one day in an Italian village and they had to take whatever lodging they could get. My friend was given an attic room and before falling asleep she heard grotesque and disquieting noises in the next room. In spite of the frightening disturbance she at last fell asleep and then had a conversation with a gentleman who was very apologetic. He said that there was nothing to be afraid of; that when he was out of his body he was quite sane, but that he could not control his body or stop it from making noises because it was insane and he was sorry it disturbed her. In the morning all this was confirmed by the lady of the house. It was her brother whom she always kept locked up. He was quite harmless, and she took him out in a wheel chair for the sun and air whenever possible. She asked that no complaint be made to the authorities, because she did not want him taken to an institution but wanted to give him what love and protection she could.

A pathetic story, especially for the cultured gentleman tied to that wretched body, but who in spite of his affliction was kind and considerate. The person who knows something of the inner side of such tragedies, is able to act as an invisible helper with such people when free from the body in sleep, and much good work is done by those who know and understand.

The Still-Born

Some students have a theory that a stillborn child may be stillborn because the review of life was missed at the previous transition. It is unlikely that there can be any truth in this idea because the review is what is elaborated between incarnations and consequently it would have little value or purpose at the conclusion of the heaven life. It must also be remembered that the new personality would be unlikely to have any ability to recall a past incarnation unless highly evolved.

Destiny Self-Created

There are some things in the indelible record of our lives that we regret having done or said. There are wrongs to be righted. They produce some degree of suffering, for how can we realize the wrongs done to others unless we know what it feels like to suffer in kind? We reap as we sow.

This digestion of experience—good, bad and indifferent—does more to refine and moralize than any other way. Certainly, precepts that are ignored help not at all. But such suffering is only temporary and acts as a wholesome purge. It can last only as long as the force we ourselves put into it, and few people are really vicious, therefore it is soon exhausted.

An understanding of this retrospect of life at death is valuable to us now because it makes us more thoughtful and deliberate as to what we do, say or think during our life on earth. It should also inspire each one to try to understand his particular plan of life for this incarnation. A man who is dissatisfied, always moving from one job to another, has not found his true work and can never be happy until he does. He will have a sense of frustration because, in his personality, he is at war with his higher self and his larger vision.

Again, if in a former life, we had spiritual opportunities and neglected them, or abused them, we may search half a lifetime before we make our contact with the Truth. We may then wonder: "Why was I not born into this Truth, or why did I not learn about it in youth?" To make sure of coming into a knowledge of Truth early in life we must not neglect what we do know now. By cultivating our present knowledge we develop an insight, and a greater penetration into that particular knowledge.

If, therefore, a person is dissatisfied with life, it means he is wandering from the path of life which he himself originally mapped out in the heaven world. Nothing in our lives is ever lost—not one job nor title shall pass away until all be fulfilled. It is fulfilled when experience culminates in wisdom. It is a wise man who does not make the same mistake twice.

Everyone will experience this marvelous review of life. Each person will find that the events of a long life, their minutest details, are marshalled in the greatest order in a few seconds of time. The afterlife then consists of the infinite developments of the various incidents and events flowing from experience. All unrealized hopes, aspirations, dreams, become fully realized. The dreams of objective life become the realities of subjective existence. We think that this earth and this material life is objective, and so it is while we are embodied, but after death the dream life becomes objective and this earth is but a shadow of a dream.

"We must live before we can attain either intelligence or control at all. We must sleep if we are not to find ourselves, at death, helplessly strange to the new conditions. And we must die before we can hope to advance to a broader understanding."*

---

* J. W. Dunne, *An Experiment with Time.*

During biscuits this morning we had occasion to think of grandpa, and lo, he turned up on a sudden and imparted a few things. We had just been having history about the protestants breaking off from the cathlics and the cathlics saying mass for the dead and all that, and we were wondering what grandpa and the spirits thought about it. Then all at once I saw old grandpa, and he said the protestants did quite wrong not to pray for people when they are what we call dead, because unselfish prayers are beautiful thoughts and make a lovely light round the spirits and help them a lot and let them know we are thinking of them too, which gives them pleasure and reminds them they are not forgotten. Grandpa said it is the parsons' fault that so many people (Protestants) don't pray for the spirits, because a lot of them make out that when we die we go to sleep till the day of resurrection, which grandpa says is all stuff and nonsense. He said when he was on earth he felt (in comparison) far more dead than alive, but now that he is supposed to be dead, he feels far more alive than dead. I've just been thinking that if mater knew about our intervues with grandpa and all he tells us, she'd think he was the devil dressed up in grandpa's clothing and come to tempt us. It does seem silly. If only mater could open herself like Mr. and Mrs. P. to things it would be so much nicer, it would really.

The Boy Who Saw True
(London: Neville Spearman, Ltd.), p. 124.
[The personal diary of a clairvoyant boy
in Victorian England]

7

HOW TO HELP

The length of an earth life depends upon the degree of the hunger for birth as well as upon our self-created destiny. For example, suppose our allotted time is eighty years but that in a former life we had been a hit-run driver who carelessly killed another. We might then be cut off by a similar accident at the age of twenty, and then reincarnate and finish our life span by an existence of sixty years. It is among such cases of rapid reincarnation that we sometimes get instances of memories of a past life.

Suicide

If a man dies prematurely by carelessness, neglect or suicide, he will remain in the atmosphere or aura of the earth until his time-period of physical life is exhausted, for that is fixed. He will be earthbound. When the earth period is ended, then the normal life after death in the astral world will begin. Most people die when the natural time comes to quit the world. It is this unpleasant condition of being earthbound which must be discussed and understood if we are to discover what happens to suicides.

First, consider the need for enlightenment. Back in 1943, the statistics stated that 50,000 people in the United States attempted suicide every year. In a copyrighted UPI story out of San Diego on 9 February 1979, it stated that the suicide rate for teenagers and young adults alone has tripled in the last 20 years, and that they have validated attempts by children as young as six or seven years old. In the thirty-six years since the above figure was given, suicide has become one of the major causes of death in the young.* Psychologists tell us that nearly everyone at one time or another considers the proposition, even if it be but a passing thought. Of the 50,000 attempts, approximately 13 percent are successful, three men to every woman. Those who read these words should surely try to introduce a little leaven to counteract this folly, because year after year the same statistics are substantially repeated.

On Being Earthbound

Our physical bodies are made up of solid, liquid, gaseous and etheric matter, but there is also a form of magnetic attraction to the earth, the result of desire to be born. Suicide destroys only the denser parts of the body—it is like plucking the

---

* In an effort to update the statistics, I was told by an official at one Suicide Prevention Bureau, that their figures reflected "successful" attempts. I recoil that any attempt which was completed can be termed a "success." Editor.

stone out of an unripe apricot or peach. It leaves a hollowed out feeling of intense unsatisfied hunger until the magnetic links with earth are worn out. There is also an intolerable heavy, leaden feeling of being perpetually tired, also due to the inability to get free from the earthbound condition. Imagine trying to walk on the street in a diver's suit. It is so heavy one can hardly lift one's feet. This weariness is caused by the pull of even a slight degree of physical gravity which the earthbound find it impossible to shake off. They usually fall into a sleep, but though they may remain unconscious for weeks, they always wake with this feeling of being distressingly tired and heavy, hardly able to move a limb. The weeks, months or years in this semi-conscious state are often broken. Especially on the anniversary of the suicide the victim may awaken to re-enact the circumstances of his premature departure from earth. This is the cause of periodical hauntings.

Dr. Carl A. Wickland, M.D., in his book, *Thirty Years Among the Dead*, tells of a couple who, in 1902, entered into a suicide pact because their parents would not permit them to marry. The girl had to urge the young man to kill her before he finally closed his eyes and shot her. Then he shot himself before he saw her fall. When he was dead he found himself alive (as everyone does) and he saw her body lying on the floor. Thinking that the suicide pact had failed and that he had killed the girl but failed to kill himself, he tried to run away, and had been running and walking ever since until 1919, when he was at last made to understand his condition, and he became sensible enough to let his dead mother take him in charge.

Another suicide said: "I have tried and tried to die but it seems every single time I come to life again." There is *no* death.

The results of suicide are infinitely worse than any possible mood of depression, or jealousy, or poverty, or shame or cowardice that might lead to it. Often the person is more or less tied to the locality of the deed and that, also, becomes a wearisome round of existence. To realize the boredom to be endured, go and stand on some street corner day and night, without any vacation for twelve months.

Cause of Hauntings

Here is a description of the post-mortem life of Guiteau, the assassin of President Garfield, as given in letters from the Masters of Wisdom. Garfield was shot in May and died in September, and his murderer was executed. "Guiteau," says the Master, "is gone into a state during the period of which he will be ever firing at his President; will ever be tried and ever hung—bathing in the reflec-

tion of thoughts and deeds, especially those in-
dulged on the scaffold."

It should be noted that this perpetual reenact-
ment of the scene and the events leading up to it is
not "forever" but only during the period of what
would have been his natural earth-life. That is bad
enough, but it will have its compensations, for the
poor victim of execution or suicide will develop
such an aversion to that particular crime that when
it is reborn on earth, he will have a conscience
which will prevent him from making that mistake
again, but that expanded conscience may not prevent his former violence of self-destruction's having its natural violent effect in his next life on
earth. His improved conscience works on its own
level, while physical violence works on its level. It
is probable that his conscience would produce a
strong premonition of violent death in some form
at the same age as his former suicide. But after that
resultant death, he would probably learn to re-
spect and value a physical body. H. P. Blavatsky
in *The Secret Doctrine*, Vol. 3 & Index (London:
Theosophical Publishing House, 1928), Section 44,
page 389, quotes Tibetan sources to the effect that
"at whatever age one puts off this outward body
by free will, at that age will he be made to die a
violent death against his will at his next rebirth."

Society commits a crime every time it permits

capital punishment. This does no good whatever, but it does result in great harm to the community. If the criminal is really vicious it sets him free to induce weak-minded people to commit crime, or as in the case of suicides, they try to get other weak-minded people to join them. Thus the famous bridge to Pasadena has claimed many victims, and those whose lives were saved testify that they were beckoned to and enticed by others who preceded them.

It is far better to substitute life imprisonment for capital punishment, because that enforced discipline is exactly what the unruly need to reform them. They don't like it; consequently, they try to avoid it in their next life on earth, and so behave as to merit parole.

In this way human beings slowly evolve. However, there is a much better and quicker way to grow; by paying attention to the advice of great teachers, like the Christ, or the Buddha, but few people are interested in that better way. They seem to insist on going through the University of Hard Knocks.

Mistaken Motives

We often hear of old people, and others afflicted with some incurable disease, who take their lives from good motives. For example—that they will not be burdens to anyone. Others, who get into financial difficulties, sometimes commit suicide so that insurance may be collected. This last is not a good motive; it is stealing from the insurance company. Two wrongs do not make a right. Anyone who accepts the proceeds of a suicide's insurance policy is living on blood money, and it would be far better for him to refuse to touch it than to profit by it. So far as not being a burden to anyone is concerned, it is not really a good motive, because we rob the family of opportunities of service and sacrifice. How do we know that the family was not responsible for exactly the conditions with which it is faced? Indeed, in numerous cases, that is proved to be the case. The acts of service we render to others will inevitably result in our own last hours being made comfortable.

If a person has cancer of the stomach and dies from that disease, or from any disease powerful enough to kill him, he is likely to be free from that disease forever, because that is its natural line of exhaustion. But if he destroys his body prematurely, his next life may find him with a cancerous body, although the disease may not be so malignant if it was almost exhausted when he committed suicide. In any case suicide is folly, because who can tell what the next moment may bring? Perhaps an instantaneous cure.

A man faced with an incurable disease or material difficulties may not see the answer and argue that he has gone too far, that he cannot overcome now at this late date, and that he will wait until he gets another body and then do better. He forgets that unless he changes his habits now, his next body will have the very same qualities and characteristics as the one he destroys. He gains nothing at all but delay, for suicide always means a return to conditions similar to those from which escape is sought.

Motives

The motive for suicide does have a great deal to do with the conditions of life after death. While all have to finish the remainder of what would have been their earth life, some remain conscious a good deal of the time and re-enact the tragedy over and over again; some sink into an uneasy slumber and only awake occasionally, to repeat the wearisome round of events leading up to their untimely death.

It is much as though a gray cloud prevents them from rising to the heaven world, and, on the other hand, they are unable to return to earth. The Christ describes this condition in almost the same terms in which modern investigators have described it. In the story of the rich man and the beggar Lazarus, the man of wealth, tantalized by water within sight but out of reach, asks Lazarus to just dip the tip of his finger in water to wet his tongue. But it is impossible because "between us and you there is a great gulf fixed" so that we cannot pass even if we would.

Suicides Are Un-Dead

This means that the fully dead cannot help the un-dead. It is necessary to have a physical body in order to be able to help suicides. When we leave our bodies at night, we can reach these poor victims of their own folly by virtue of the fact that we are still linked with earth, the silver cord not yet being broken.

It is necessary to have a physical body to be able to help the suicide because he is still magnetically linked to the earth. A person who dies at his allotted time may be earth-bound for a time by worry, but this is a very different condition from that of the earth-bound suicide, who feels desperately tired and heavy because of the pull of physical gravity.

But when we die to earth the silver cord is severed, and we have then no means of grasping the magnetic attraction of the semi-physical.

We have already explained that the reason suicides cannot be free to go on for the remnant of their natural earth-life is that, like everyone else who is born on earth, their initial thirst for physical life must first be exhausted. It is this hunger or thirst for earthly experience which drives us to seek birth into the world. This is the cause which determines the duration of the earth-bound condition. The original desire of the immortal soul for physical life cannot be canceled by the subordinate mortal personality, and it is this restless craving which keeps the suicides awake and surrounded with creations of imagination in which they live for months or years, as the case may be. It is not a question of punishment, for nature deals only with consequences; with cause and effect. And this all-pervading law of divine justice is infinitely kind and merciful. God's plan for man is unending progress.

The condition of suicides is just as varied as the condition of all other people in the life after death, within self-created limitations. So it is true for them as for all people; "In my Father's House are many mansions."

Helping the Suicide

The best help we can render the suicide, if we find ourselves in communication with him, is to induce him to cease all efforts to get back into the physical world. If a man has given way to drink on earth and is now earth-bound, he will try to smell and to taste liquor by obsessing a drinker, thus achieving a vicarious satisfaction. There would be a good deal less drinking and over-eating and sexual excess if people could see the thirsty "dead drunks" hanging around bars, and the libertines seeking sensuous satisfaction through the bodies of others. One ought to be fairly free from temptation oneself in order to undertake to help a suicide. Often, when a suicide has attached himself to a living person of his own type, he complains that he "can't get rid of that gross fellow," and imagines that the living person is obsessing *him*. It is in many ways a fifty-fifty proposition and it requires a strong will to break it, but most of such people are weak-willed. The obsessing connection can be broken by an exorcism, but ultimately each person must develop his own will power, in order to be master of his own body.

Since the departed live in a world of thought and feeling, the most potent help we can give is uplifting, serene emotion, and the calm power of thought. Suppose our victim of folly is active, and struggling to get a foothold in the world he has left. The constant blessing he receives, as he is remembered in thought, will enable him to get a better perspective of his situation, will bring him some measure of peace; and in the light of that peace and knowledge he will gradually stop making a bad matter worse. As his natural span of life draws to a close he may spend more time in unconsciousness, and only awaken to the unpleasant consequences of his act, as its anniversary comes around and his memory becomes vivid again.

If our suicide has fallen into the unconscious

condition of slumber, the blessing and kindly thought of friends will be stored up in his aura, ready to discharge its helpful benediction at his natural death hour, and so carry him into the heaven world with less of a handicap. Good wishes and prayers have the effect of acting as a shield or protection against any selfish or ignorant people who want to communicate with the suicide.

From every point of view suicide is folly. It solves no problem, but merely postpones the solution. We can render enormous and fruitful service if only we understand the varied conditions of life after death, and put that knowledge into practice.

When the natural death hour arrives and the restraining magnetic ties with earth are finally severed, the suicide feels a marvelous sense of freedom. All the tired weariness drops away and he at last feels the lightness and buoyancy of the newly dead. From then on he is restored to his natural course of evolution, which has been interrupted by his mistake.

Even those who previously had some traditional conviction about the nature of the afterlife world seem to have moved away from it to some degree following their own brushes with death. In fact, in all the reports I have gathered, not one person has painted the mythological picture of what lies hereafter. None has described the cartoonist's heaven of pearly gates, golden streets, and winged harp-playing angels, not a hell of flames and demons with pitchforks.

So, in most cases, the reward-punishment model of the afterlife is abandoned and disavowed, even by the many who had been accustomed to thinking in those terms. They found, much to their amazement, that even when their most apparently awful and sinful deeds were made manifest before the being of light, the being responded not with anger and rage, but rather only with understanding, and even with humor.

Raymond A. Moody, Jr., *Life After Life*
(N.Y.: Bantam Books, 1975).

8

THE MOMENT AFTER TRANSITION

There is no rigid uniformity in the experience of people immediately after death. Some do not know they are dead; some fall into a dreamless sleep; some feel a sense of triumph and freedom which thrills their entire being once they are finally separated from their bodies. Our best plan will be to describe typical examples of varying experiences.

The Etheric Double After Death

During earth life the etheric double is conterminous with the nervous system as well as enveloping it. In outline, in form and feature, it is a replica or double of the physical body in matter finer and more tenuous than the finest gaseous substance, yet it is still physical matter. When it is withdrawn by means of the silver cord at transition it is called the shade or shell. A person who understands the inner nature of man drops it immediately it is disconnected from the nervous system. He is then free in his astral body. The etheric double disintegrates or dematerializes once it is abandoned. It never was intended to be a vehicle of consciousness. Its function was to convey vitality to the body through the nervous system. But people who have no knowledge of the inner nature of man often try to cling to it, and so long as they do, it may appear as an apparition or ghost. Its appearance is that of a bluish-white mist. If cremation takes place while a person is clinging to the etheric counterpart, this will immediately destroy it. The average time people remain in it is from ten minutes to thirty hours. If they do, they remain asleep or unconscious, under normal conditions, and when they awake there is nowhere but the astral world they can awake to, because the physical body is dead when the silver cord is broken and there is no getting back into it. Death means that the etheric double is disunited from the nervous system, but the double is no more to be preserved than the physical is; it is part of the physical and will disintegrate.

Immediately on awakening in the astral world the etheric matter fades out like mist. The last contact with physical matter is at an end. Once the man is free from etheric matter there is nothing to hold the double together.

Do Not Injure the Dead

This period of unconsciousness after transition is a merciful arrangement of nature because one is not distressed by the emotional disturbance of relatives who may mourn and weep. So long as people are ignorant we have to allow for a certain amount of grief, but it causes injury to the newly dead, and it is therefore a good thing for them to be unconscious of it, exactly as in sleep.

The period immediately after death is a restful state such as one experiences after a good night's sleep—a condition between waking and sleeping. It should not be disturbed by violent weeping. One of the hardest burdens the newly dead have to bear is the unbelief of friends and relatives. A man who can think a person is dead because his physical body is still and dead becomes hermetically sealed against any contact with the newly dead.

Death liberates the real man and unfolds his inner senses. What is there in this to cause grief? Only one's own selfish feeling of loss.

There are various ways of awakening people from this period of unconsciousness. Frequently friends who have previously passed on watch for a suitable time when the emotional disturbance of the so-called living has sufficiently subsided. This suitable time often arises when those in physical bodies fall asleep, but it may be possible to wake up the newly dead within ten or fifteen minutes if the relatives are fairly sensible. The etheric double then disintegrates. If left to himself the average person would awaken within a few hours. One effective means to achieve freedom from the etheric double in sacramental churches is the Absolution of the Dead, which should be given as soon after death as possible. The effect of this, so far as the etheric double is concerned, is to loosen and expel any remaining etheric matter from the body, to make certain that the silver cord is broken and to get the person completely free from the etheric double so that it disintegrates.

Without this help of Absolution, or some other form of outside assistance, it is advisable to leave the physical body in peace for a few hours, especially in the case of people who know nothing of the things we are discussing.

Cremation

No one need fear cremation because it is quite impossible for a dead person to feel effects of the fire on his discarded body, for death means that both etheric and astral matter have been completely separated from the physical. The silver cord being severed there is no way in which sensation can be conveyed.

The Unconvinced Dead

There are some very materialistic people who try to cling desperately to the physical body. They may awaken still surrounded by etheric matter. In that case they are suspended between the physical and the astral worlds, yet shut out from both. They drift about in what seems to them a thick and gloomy fog. Sometimes a rift will come in this etheric fog and they catch a glimpse first of the physical world, and then of the astral. In time the etheric sheath finally wears out and they are free. There are those in the invisible world who make it their job to help free these ignorant people.

Now let us take a case where the man does not know that he is dead. In the first place, he has not passed through death to life in unbroken consciousness. He has his period of dreamless sleep, but when he awakens he finds himself in a part of the astral world wherein all material objects are duplicated in finer matter. He is unable to distinguish any difference, yet presently he notes some puzzling facts. The best way to understand this is to relate the experience of one intelligent man who firmly believed that there could be no other life than that of this earth.

In the course of time he died, as we all must. After an interval he encountered a friend of mine (still living on earth) who had extra-sensory perception. The "dead" man said: "Something strange has happened to me. You know, I was sick for a long time, in fact expected to die, but I didn't; I have completely recovered and am as well and strong as ever. But there are things I cannot understand. I go home and no one takes any notice of me. It is really insulting. I sit in my accustomed arm chair and someone has the impertinence to sit down through me. I go down to the bank and find that I can go right in whether the doors are open or not. I can't make it out at all. I know I am not dead. You can see that for yourself. So I must be still living, yet these strange things happen to me. I have thought it all over carefully and I have come to the conclusion that while I am fully recovered from my illness, my brain must have been affected and I am crazy."

My friend was able to explain that it was not so bad as all that; that the troubled man was alive and sane but that his physical body was as dead as a salt mackerel. It is not so easy to convince such a man but it can be done with patience and logic.

Indignant at Being Alive

There are many cases like this with varying degrees of stubbornness. A materialist who was very dogmatic during life may be so determined to be dead and unconscious that he may remain in a state of deep unconsciousness for weeks and months. When they finally awake, such people are usually indignant at first at finding themselves alive. They may then say: "Well, I admit I was wrong. There is another form of life, but there is nothing beyond *this*." There are many who fight natural progress every inch of the way, just as there are many on earth who answer the demonstrable facts of psychical research by denying the evidence and ignoring the facts.

Many of those killed in accidents, many suicides, many soldiers killed suddenly, do not know immediately that they are dead.

"Am I Dreaming?"

Those also who die after prolonged illness cannot believe that they are dead. It is a common experience in dying to wake and find oneself alive and well. The first idea with many is that they are dreaming, because they recollect that they have gone to sleep many times but always they have awakened to physical pain. One day they wake and find themselves entirely free from pain, so the first thought is that they are dreaming; but as the dream goes on and on, the second thought is that an instantaneous, miraculous cure has taken place. They have heard of sudden healings but never expected it to happen to them. There is naturally a feeling of delight as well as a sensation of lightness and bouyancy. The next thing that happens to such a person is that he sees his physical body lying still and dead and he observes the actions of the nurse or relatives. Then he thinks: "I suppose I'm dead! I didn't expect it to be anything like this. I feel fine."

"Christian" Expectations!

What does the average person expect? His expectations are usually pretty vague and inarticulate. Many take the position that they will wait until they are dead to find out. The expectations of the average guilt-ridden, orthodox Christian are

more definite. He expects to go to hell and meet the
devil. That is what he has heard about all his life
and that has been called the Gospel. (The word
gospel means *"good news!"*) But if the departed
has been somewhat of a reprobate during his life,
and someone has induced him to accept a particular theology at the eleventh hour, then he expects
to go to heaven. We will deal later with the facts
about Heaven, Hell and Purgatory. Mark Twain
reduces this "salvation by belief" theory to its logical absurdity when divorced from a corresponding sincerity of action. First he describes a drunkard and then draws a picture of the rejoicing in
heaven over the so-called reformed drunkard—the
procession of saints and angels who meet the
repentant sinner with bands and harps and trum-
pets, and how our reprobate meets Abraham,
Isaac and Jacob—and, falling on their necks,
weeps maudlin tears of joy. There are so many
people who spend their lives on the principle of
"eat, drink and be merry," and then accept an in-
tellectually bankrupt theology at the eleventh
hour, that Mark Twain says that Abraham, Isaac
and Jacob must be wet as muskrats most of the
time!

The Dead Convinced at Last

The newly dead person does not find himself in
either heaven or hell. He finds that the whole phys-

ical world is duplicated in finer matter; substance more ethereal. That is why he cannot tell the difference immediately. The relatives look at the dead body. All their attention is centered on it. To the newly dead it looks like an abandoned dwelling, falling to pieces. It seems absurd to him to concentrate so much attention on that when he stands there alive and well. But they, not having super sensory perception, cannot see, or feel or hear him. When he speaks it is as though a soundproof double glass separates them. When he puts out his hand to touch them, it goes through their bodies as though it was a warm fog. To us, a person in his astral body is nothing but a transparent cloud, although every feature is clearly recognizable. To the dead, a physical body is like a moist clammy fog.

When the newly dead see that there is nothing to be done with the uncomprehending living, they turn their attention away to the astral world, and usually they find friends and relatives ready to welcome them. In fact, those who have passed on before are often observed before death takes place, and the pleasure of recognition is a big factor in making transition a delightful process. One is very soon much more interested in the astral world than one is in trying to renew contact with the physical. It is much the same feeling as a traveler has when pulling into a foreign port. He remembers the

homeland but for the time being his attention is
concentrated on new scenes, old friends and more
interesting events than a dead physical body for
which he has as little use as for an old suit he plans
to burn in the incinerator. His sense of relative
values is completely reversed.

Dead Attend the Funeral

There are many people to whom the discovery
of life after death comes as a great shock. This is
true especially if they have had wealth and have
been able to buy their way through life; if they
have been in domineering positions of command—
all this avails nothing in the process of dying and
in life after death. All are on the same democratic
basis. There is no favored class. As *Life* once put
it: "All are on a spirit-level!"

A good deal has been said against the barbarous
custom of black clothes, elaborate funerals, and
other conventional outward signs of mourning.
But in the case of self-satisfied materialists, these
are useful, because they advertise to a man that he
is dead. In such cases it is a good thing to have a
long drawn-out funeral and a lot of fuss. Many
people attend their own funerals, and it is just as
well to induce the dead man to wait around for an
hour or so listening to eulogies and compliments
about his virtues. Gradually the advertising begins

to take effect. It dawns upon him that he must be dead. He knows his friends would not say such nice things about him if he were alive. He never received so many flowers in all his life. He therefore concludes that he is dead. That turns his attention and interest away; by the time he thinks once more of the funeral it is all over and his friends are eating light refreshments back at home. He may then hear some things that were not in the eulogies. For example: "Why in the world did he make a will like that?"

When a man dies, if he has no interests other than those of a material nature, he is in poverty—he has laid up no treasures on the other side. He cannot return. His hope of progress now depends on being deprived of his trumpery material possessions. The discovery of the utter nothingness of the important things of earth is one of the extraordinary experiences of dying. It really helps such a man to see his fortune go smash, if necessary, and not be able to put a finger out to control it. These things are often summed up in a single line of scripture. "A man's life does not consist in the abundance of the things he possesses." It really consists of character. That is the only wealth with which we come into the world and the only treasure we can take out of it. Without character we stumble and fall and injure ourselves in the darkness of ignorance; with character and wisdom the problems of life melt away; we find our true selves, the higher selves, and we may learn to control not only the manner of our dying but our life after death, and the birth of our next incarnation.

The more I observe and study things, the more convinced I become that sorrow over separation and death is perhaps the greatest delusion. To realize that it is a delusion is to become free. There is no death, no separation of the substance.

Mohandas K. Gandhi, *Letters to a Disciple*

9

WHY MOURN?

It comes as a shock to many people when it is pointed out that the widespread attitude of mourning, especially if made into a public display, is essentially selfish. They do not think of themselves as selfish at all but sincerely believe that they are being ordinarily human and decent, and that it would be unnatural and cold-hearted if they did not express grief and sorrow.

With these considerations in mind, we shall deal gently with mourning customs, although all will surely agree that some of them are barbaric, insincere and hypocritical, and cannot be defended. For example, in *Psalms* 56, verse 8, it is said, "Put thy tears into thy tear bottle." This refers to a Jewish mourning custom whereby professional mourners were hired to weep. But in order to prevent cheating they had to collect the tears into little bottles, and these bottles were then sealed and placed in the tomb. In various modern museums some of these tear bottles may be seen. They are **small** vials about the length and thickness of a finger of the hand. The more tears collected the greater was the satisfaction of the family, even though the tears were bought and paid for. The fifth column in France used this method to break down the morale before the victorious Germans knocked France out of the war. Women dressed in black went about weeping over fictitious war losses, with the result that many men became depressed and were willing to lose honor and country before they would give their lives in defense of country.

Roman Customs

In ancient Roman times, if a dead Roman did not have a large assortment of women relatives to weep for him, female mourners were hired; the fees depended on the service rendered. If the mourners simply followed the bier in silence, they received about four cents each; if required to weep, the fee was six cents; shrieking and loud cries and lamentations, together with tearing of the hair, beating the breast and other signs of extreme grief, cost the afflicted relatives fifteen cents for each industrious mourner. At the funeral of Titus fifteen hundred professional mourners were employed, all at the highest prices.

Irish Custom

The Irish wake is another example of artificial grief. The corpse is laid out on the bed in full sight, and the mourners fill the house and remain all night. They talk and smoke and have refreshments, including a large barrel of porter or other similar forms of drink. As the night wears on they become a little befuddled. Several times during the night the women join arms in a circle around the corpse, wailing and bending over, and this crying and screaming may go on for fifteen minutes at a time. It is called "ulogone." It is usually started by one woman during a pause in the refreshments, and others join; there are women who acquire quite a reputation for wailing. They will say: "Mrs. O'Flanagan is wonderful for ulogone," somewhat in the way a good cheer leader is in demand at a ball game.

Chinese Customs

There is a Chinese proverb which says: "You cannot prevent the birds of sorrow from flying over your head, but you can prevent them from building nests in your hair." That proverb shows that there are Chinese who do not approve of unrestrained mourning.

Yet the usual Chinese funeral is a constant succession of efforts to cheat the devil. The departed is safe so long as the body remains in the house; the risk begins when the funeral procession starts, therefore firecrackers and a smoke screen are started at the door; under cover of this, the pallbearers start off at a lively trot, run to the nearest corner, and make a sharp turn. The reason for this is that the devil cannot negotiate turns quickly. By setting off more firecrackers at the corner the devil is confused still more. In this way, by a series of quick turns they reach the cemetery, but they do not go in through the gate but through a gap in the hedge or wall, because they know the baffled devil is waiting at the gate. Once in the cemetery they feel reasonably safe, but to make sure they set off more firecrackers until the rites are ended.

"Christian" Materialism

All this must seem to the average American nothing but superstition, as indeed it is. The devil does not seem to get a square deal, for no allowance is made for his stupidity. But is the attitude of mind so very different from that of the fundamentalists? They also expect to go to hell and meet the devil; they also weep and cry out excessively and wear long black clothes; and the clergy use black vestments, a black catafalque and yellow funeral candles; all is gloom.

The Ideal Attitude

What then is the ideal attitude to adopt in the face of death? That attitude will be determined by our knowledge of the truth concerning life after death. But the truth which leads us to deplore and seek to correct the false and the superstitious and the selfish does not mean an attitude of coldness or a callous disregard of tender feelings. On the contrary, it makes us more understanding and sympathetic. There ought to be no gloom about a funeral nor need there be.

The first step in knowledge is to cast aside the vague, materialistic conception that man has a soul. Reverse the idea by saying that man *is* a soul and has a body. The body is but a garment, and what we call death is but the laying aside of a worn out garment. It is no more the end of mind and soul than it is the end of the body when we remove an overcoat. Therefore, to imagine that death means that we have lost our friend is a delusion. Our friend has put aside his body, but he has not ceased to exist. The sorrow and the mourning arise from disbelief or doubt of the truth. The degree of grief is the measure of unbelief. St. Paul says: "I would not have you ignorant concerning them that are asleep, that ye sorrow not, even as others who have no hope."

"I Am Not Dead"

One of the hardest blows we give to the departed is to think of them as dead when it is more than likely that they are standing right beside us. The so-called dead look with amazement and won-

der and chagrin at people mourning and weeping
over the abandoned body. They ask themselves
what all the fuss is about. "I am *not* dead," one
says, somewhat indignantly, "My body is gone, it
is true, but *I* am not my body." He thinks: "What a
grotesque idea!" Yet the departed person forgets
that he also had the same materialistic delusion
when he was *in* the body. The remedy is to acquire
knowledge before the event occurs, not to wait until we are suddenly face to face with death, and
then feel crushed by it in sorrow, grief, weeping
and mourning. There is no virtue in ignorance.

Let me tell you a true story related to me by the
president of a university. He said that his younger
sister was happily married and had one child,
a boy of four years. Their mother had died when
the sister was too young to remember her, consequently she was not familiar with the physical appearance of her mother. One day she was in the
nursery with the child, and saw standing in the
doorway her father, who was also dead, and
whom she knew very well. At his side was an
elderly lady.

The astral father said: "My dear, this is your
mother. You were too young to remember her, as
she died when you were a small child." Then he
said: "In four days we shall take Robin and look
after him for you."

Now, the little boy, Robin, was quite well; there was nothing wrong with him, no defect of any kind. This incident occurred in the late morning. At noon the husband came in for lunch and his wife related the experience. As is usual with many people he made light of it and passed it off as "imagination." But within four days the boy became sick and did die. The president of the university concluded the story by saying: "It was a strange thing, but my sister never wept or mourned. She was confident that her father and mother were looking after Robin."

I said to this college president: "What is the use of having a department devoted to psychology when it ignores the facts of life and death?"

He replied: "It is futile."

Forearmed with Knowledge

The loss of a loved one need not be hard. There could not well be a closer bond of affection than that between a young mother and a little child. The difficulty is that people wait until the blow falls, suddenly and unexpectedly, while they are in complete ignorance of the facts of life after death, and then they expect to be comforted in their ignorance. The time to arm oneself against such blows is long before they fall. Then, when one is face to face with the dead body, he knows his loved one is not a body but the dweller in the body. Consider the origin of the word "body," the Anglo-Saxon word "bodig," meaning an abode or dwelling. That is what the physical body is. Those who act upon that knowledge do not mourn and weep when a loved one is released from the body which has served its purpose well. When there has been pain and suffering what kind of love is it which would bind a loved one to that torture, merely for the selfish satisfaction of seeing weariness and labored breathing? Still worse is the selfishness that would unconsciously try to bind a living person, free in his more glorious astral body, to a dead physical body for which he has no use whatever.

For one who knows that the body is not the real man, grief does not exist. It exists only for the unconvinced or the half-convinced, that is, for the materialist. But, you say, even the materialist needs comfort. True enough, but the way to give that comfort is not to agree weakly and dishonestly with his ignorance. It is by giving him the knowledge whereby his mourning and weeping is overcome so that he ceases to injure his loved one by his black despair and depression. Yes, we know quite well that the death of a loved one is one of the hardest things in life to bear. But one touch of knowledge rolls away the grief and sorrow as if it were a stone at the door of a sepulcher. And if one is fortunate enough, and sensitive enough, to see the astral body, the vividness of that experience is indescribable. The dead physical body becomes unimportant and all mourning ceases.

Mourning a Direful Influence

Because the dead are far better off than we are, having passed to a much wider life, it is not necessary to sympathize with them. With friends and relatives who mourn the loss we do sympathize because they cannot see or believe the truth. The grief of friends attracts the attention of the dead, just as a crying child draws our attention, and this tends to draw the departed again into touch with earth. It is cruel to draw to earth one who yearns to be free. It interrupts his progress to try to arouse in him any desire for further earthly life which he has left. The very fact that he has affection for us, and sympathy for us, lays him open to this direful influence we pour upon him. Instead of using the power of our sympathy and affection to injure him, we can use it to help him. We must forget ourselves and think of him in terms of godspeed. Since every thought and feeling of ours reaches him, we should take care that we are not self-centered but helpful and generous.

The cause of our mourning and grief is therefore delusion. Our friends are not dead though "in the sight of the unwise they seem to die, and their departure is taken for misery, and their going from us to be utter destruction; but they are in peace, for God created man to be immortal, and made him to be an image of his own eternity."* There is plenty of evidence that this, and not materialism, is the truth

When we stop thinking of ourselves, and consequently mourning *our* loss, we may begin to think what we can do to help the departed. There are some who seem to think it is wrong to pray for the dead. What a curious mental aberration. If it is a sign of love to think with affection of an absent friend on the side of the earth, why should it suddenly become a sin to stop loving him merely because his body is dead? "Prayer is the heart's sincere desire, uttered or unexpressed." So the question arises, once we have stopped the mourning which only injures our loved one, how can we help the departed?

The Best Prayer

The prayer of the Liberal Catholic Church gives a complete answer: "Rest in the Eternal, grant unto him, O Lord. And let the perpetual light shine upon him." It is dreadful to be earthbound, so the first care should be to give our loved one rest from all earthly worries and cares. When he sees that we

---

* Liberal Catholic Liturgy.

are determined to face life and do our best to solve its problems, then the departed ceases to be worried and can even help us. Opportunities may come our way unexpectedly, and the solution of how to go on without our loved one may often be one that had not previously entered our mind. In the higher consciousness we can see much farther than the limitation of the brain permits, but this wider vision cannot penetrate so long as we are preoccupied with our own grief.

The second part of the ancient prayer is that our loved one, being held to earth no longer, may have uninterrupted light upon the pathway of his new and free life. There are people who say: "My loved one can never be happy unless I am with him." Here again they are thinking in terms of materialism. We are with our departed friends when we sleep, and often we remember that contact as a vivid dream. It has occurred often that a departed person has given information to someone on earth. Dante, having died, told his son where to find a manuscript. But it would be exceedingly selfish to have insisted that Dante remain in lower realms near the earth when the wide vistas of the heaven world were open before him. The proper thing to do is to so purify our natures that we are capable of rising in consciousness to their higher level, rather than drag our friends down to ours.

If we say we believe in immortality let it not be

idle talk. If **we** say we are convinced of continued existence, then we have no right to stand by an abandoned body and grieve as though **we** were not convinced. To those whom death has left desolate let us call attention to the words of the great teacher, Shri Krishna:

> "Thou Grievest where no grief should be!
> Thou speakest words lacking wisdom! for the
> wise in heart
> Mourn not for those that live, nor those that
> die.
> Nor I, nor thou, nor any one of those,
> Ever was not, nor ever will not be
> For ever and for ever afterwards.
> All, that doth live, lives always!
> Never the spirit was born; the spirit shall cease
> to be never;
> Never was time it was not; end and beginning
> are dreams.
> Birthless and deathless and changeless remain-
> eth the spirit forever,
> Death hath not touched it at all, dead though
> the house of it seems!"
> > Sir Edwin Arnold, *The Song Celestial*

EPIGRAPH

Is death only the beginning of a far more fantastic state of existence than life? Lyall Watson thinks it is, and he describes our traditional view of death as an error of perception, like Romeo's tragic misunderstanding of Juliet's apparent lifelessness.

This is the "THE ROMEO ERROR", and its key lies in natural history: "Life evolved from the non-living and still depends for its efficient survival on the non-survival of some of its parts. Life and death are indistinguishable, but there is a third and distinct state of growth and a clearly defined series of events which lead to it. These can be manifest at any time of life.

"What we call death is merely a change of state, often temporary and sometimes curable. Death on its own has no clinical, logical, or biological reality and exists only as a construct with validity in interpersonal relationships.

"When Romeo found Juliet pale and lifeless in the tomb and assumed she was dead, she *was* dead. The fact that she later recovered and became more lifelike does not cancel out her death. When Juliet found Romeo lying lifeless with poison in his hand, he too was dead and his death would remain valid even if some quickwitted physician has rushed in from the wings and pumped out his stomach in the nick of time. The Romeo Error is all in the mind."

. . . little doubt that there is far more to both life and

death than we are able to comprehend by the poor evidence of our five senses—that in fact the two may be indistinguishable, with what we call death merely a change of state, often temporary and sometimes even curable.

Lyall Watson, *The Romeo Error*
(N.Y.: Doubleday, 1975).

BIBLIOGRAPHY

Arundale, George S. *The Night Bell.* Adyar: Theosophical Publishing House, 1940.

_____. *You.* Adyar: Theosophical Publishing House, 1956.

Arnold, Sir Edwin. *Death And Afterwards.* London: Trubner, 1889.

Barker, Elsa. *Letters From A Living Dead Man.* N.Y.: Mitchell Kennerly, 1915.

Bendit, Laurence J. *The Mirror Of Life And Death.* Wheaton: Theosophical Publishing House, 1965.

Besant, Annie. *The Ancient Wisdom.* Adyar: Theosophical Publishing House, 1966.

_____. *Death And After.* Benares: Theosophical Publishing House, 1901.

_____. *Man's Life In This And Other Worlds.* Adyar: Theosophical Publishing House, 1913.

_____. *Talks With A Class.* Chicago: Theosophical Press, 1922.

Blavatsky, H. P. *H. P. Blavatsky Collected Writings, Vol. V.* Adyar: Theosophical Publishing House, 1950.

_____. *The Key To Theosophy.* Wheaton: Theosophical Publishing House, 1973.

Brandon, Wilfred. *Open The Door.* N.Y.: C. & R. Anthony, 1969.

Bruteau, Beatrice. *Evolution Toward Divinity.* Wheaton: Theosophical Publishing House, 1974.

Budge, E. A. Wallis. *Egyptian Book Of The Dead.* N.Y.: Dover, 1967.

Burt, Lawrence W. *Do The Dead Suffer?* Adyar: Theosophical Publishing House, 1939.

Campbell, Joseph, ed. *Man And Transformation, Vol. 5.* Eranos Yearbooks, Bollingen Series, No. 30, 1964.

Carrington, H. *The Case For Psychic Survival.* N.Y.: Citadel Press, 1957.

_____, and Meader, John R. *Death, Its Causes And Phenomena, With Special Reference to Immortality*. London: William Rider & Son, 1911.

Cerminara, Gina. *Insights For The Age of Aquarius*. Wheaton: Theosophical Publishing House, 1976.

Codd, Clara M. *The Ageless Wisdom Of Life*. Wheaton: Theosophical Publishing House, 1967.

_____. *Trust Yourself To Life*. Wheaton: Theosophical Publishing House, 1975.

_____. *There Is No Death*. Auckland: New Zealand Section, 1952.

Collins, Mabel. *When The Sun Moves Northward*. London: Theosophical Publishing House, 1923.

Crookall, Robert. *During Sleep*. London: Theosophical Publishing House, 1964.

_____. *Events On The Threshold Of The After-Life*. Moradavard, India: Darshara International, 1967.

de Purucker, G. *The Esoteric Tradition, Vol. 11*. Covina, CA: Theosophical University Press, 1935.

de Zirkoff, Boris, ed. *Hypnotism-Mesmerism And Reincarnation*. Los Angeles: Blavatsky Writings Publication Fund, 1956.

Deathbed Observations By Physicians And Nurses. N.Y.: Parapsychology Foundation, 1961.

Evans-Wentz, W. Y. *The Tibetan Book Of The Dead*. N.Y.: Oxford University Press, 1960.

Farthing, G. *Exploring The Great Beyond*. Wheaton: Theosophical Publishing House, 1978.

Fausset, Hugh L'Anson. *Fruits Of Silence*. N.Y.: Abelard-Schuman, 1963.

Gardner, E. L. *The Nature And Function Of The Soul*. London: Theosophical Publishing House, 1946.

Garrett, Eileen J. *Does Man Survive Death?* N.Y.: Helix Press, 1957.

Hall, Manly P. *Death And After*. Los Angeles: Philosophical Research Society.

Hodson, Geoffrey. *Clairvoyant Research And The Life After Death.* London: Theosophical Publishing House, 1958.

———. *The Call To The Heights.* Wheaton: Theosophical Publishing House, 1975.

———. *Lecture Notes, Vol. I.* Adyar: Theosophical Publishing House, 1962.

———. *Through The Gateway Of Death.* Adyar: Theosophical Publishing House, 1953.

Jinarajadasa, C. *The Early Teachings Of The Masters.* Chicago: Theosophical Press, 1923.

Johnson, George L. *The Great Problems And The Evidence For Its Solution.* London: Hutchinson, 1927.

Johnson, Raynor C. *The Imprisoned Splendour.* London: Hodder & Soughton, 1954.

———. *Nurslings Of Immortality.* N.Y.: Harper Bros., 1957.

———. *A Religious Outlook For Modern Man.* N.Y.: McGraw-Hill, 1963.

Judge, William Q. *The Ocean Of Theosophy.* Los Angeles: United Lodge of Theosophists, 1928.

Krishnamurti, J. *Commentaries On Living, 3rd. Series.* Edited by D. Rajagopal. Wheaton: Theosophical Publishing House, 1960.

Kubler-Ross, Elisabeth. *On Death And Dying.* N.Y.: Macmillan Publishing Co., 1974.

———. *Death: The Final Stage Of Growth.* N.Y.: Prentice-Hall, 1975.

Leadbeater, C. W. *The Astral Plane.* Adyar: Theosophical Publishing House, 1970.

———. *The Devachanic Plane.* London: Theosophical Publishing House, 1909.

———. *The Hidden Side Of Things.* Adyar: Theosophical Publishing House, 1974.

———. *The Inner Life, Vol. 11.* Adyar: Theosophical Publishing House, 1942.

———. *The Life After Death.* Adyar: Theosophical Publishing House, 1964.

_____. *Invisible Helpers*. London: Theosophical Publishing House, 1928.

_____. *The Other Side Of Death*. Adyar: Theosophical Publishing House, 1961.

_____. *A Textbook Of Theosophy*. Los Angeles: Theosophical Publishing House, 1918.

Lodge, Sir Oliver. *Conviction Of Survival*. London: Methuen, 1930.

MacGregor, Geddes. *Reincarnation In Christianity*. Wheaton: Theosophical Publishing Press, 1978.

Maeterlinck, Maurice. *The Light Beyond*. N.Y.: Dodd Mead, 1977.

Moody, Jr., Raymond A. *Life After Death*. N.Y.: Bantam Books, 1977.

_____. *Reflections On Life After Life*. N.Y.: Bantam Books, 1978.

Myers, F. W. H. *Human Personality And Its Survival Of Bodily Death, 2 Vols*. London: Longmans Green, 1920.

Of Death And Dying. The American Theosophist, Special Issue, Spring, 1973.

Osborne, Arthur W. *The Meaning Of Personal Existence*. Wheaton: Theosophical Publishing House, 1966.

Pavri, P. *Theosophy Explained*. Adyar: Theosophical Publishing House, 1925.

Payne, Phoebe D., and Bendit, L. J. *This World And That*. London: Faber & Faber, 1950.

Pearson, E. Norman. *Space, Time And Self*. Wheaton: Theosophical Publishing House, 1967.

Pelgrin, M. *And A Time To Die*. Wheaton: Theosophical Publishing House, 1976.

Perkins, James S. *Through Death To Rebirth*. Wheaton: Theosophiical Publishing House, 1961.

Podmore, Frank. *The Naturalisation Of The Supernatural*. London: G. P. Putnam's Sons, 1908.

Powell, A. E. *The After-Death Life*. London: Besant & Co., 1929.

————. *The Astral Body.* London: Theosophical Publishing House, 1972.

————. *The Causal Body And The Ego.* London: Theosophical Publishing House, 1928.

————. *The Mental Body.* London: Theosophical Publishing House, 1975.

Prem, Sri Krishna. *The Yoga Of The Kathopanishad.* London: John M. Watkins, 1955.

Ram, N. Sri. *Thoughts For Aspirants.* Wheaton: Theosophical Publishing House, 1972.

Ramacharaka, Yogi. *Life Beyond Death.* Chicago: Yoga Publication Society.

Rogers, L. W. *Elementary Theosophy.* Wheaton: Theosophical Publishing House, 1968.

————. *Reincarnation And Other Lectures.* Chicago: Theo Book Co., 1925.

Savage, Minot J. *Life Beyond Death.* N.Y.: G. F. Putnam's Sons, 1901.

Scott-Elliot, W. *Man's Place In The Universe.* London: Theosophical Publishing House, 1902.

Shearman, Hugh. *Modern Theosophy.* Adyar: Theosophical Publishing House, 1962.

Sinnett, A. P. *Esoteric Buddhism.* Boston: Houghton Mifflin, 1912.

Stead, W. T. *After Death, A Personal Narrative.* N.Y.: George H. Doran, 1914.

Steiner, Rudolf. *Investigations In Occultism.* N.Y.: Putnam, 1920.

————. *Life Between Death And Rebirth.* N.Y.: Steiner Books (Multimedia).

————. *An Outline Of Occult Science.* N.Y.: Rand, McNally, 1914.

Thomas, L. "Notes of A Biology-Watcher". In *New England Journal of Medicine,* Vol. 288, January 11, 1973.

Watson, Lyall. *The Romeo Error: A Meditation On Life And Death.* N.Y.: Dell, 1976.

Weatherhead, Leslie D. *Life Begins At Death*. Nashville: Abingdon, 1970.

White, Stewart Edward. *The Betty Book*. N.Y.: E. P. Dutton, 1943.

Williams, Bertha. *Living On A Star*. Wheaton: Theosophical Publishing House, 1946.

Wilson, William. *After-Life, The Diagnosis Of A Physician*. London: Rider.

Wood, E. *Questions On Occultism*. Edited by Kwaku Adzei. Wheaton: Theosophical Publishing House, 1978.